Debbie
Welcome to the
thin veil. May this
book help you through
so many of the losses of
precious animals.
Beatrice Lydecker

# WALKING THE THIN VEIL

**Beatrice Lydecker-Hayford**

**PRESS**

# Table of Contents

# Introduction

"Eye hath not seen, nor ear heard, neither have entered
into the heart of man, the things which God hath
prepared for them that love him."
I Corinthians 2:9


"For we see but a poor reflection; then we shall see
face to face; Now I know in part; then shall I know
fully,
even as also I am fully known."
I Corinthians 13:12

These are exciting passages giving us something to look forward to when we step out of
our bodies for the last time, but is that all we can know
about the "other dimension?" What about now? Is there
another *reality* existing along with the physical world

we presently experience? Is what we can see, feel and encounter the only dimension that presently exists? I do not believe it is. The things I have experienced during my 75 years of living on Planet Earth have shown me that the physical and spiritual worlds exist side-by-side with only a very THIN VEIL separating them. Many of us often encounter that "other side," but because we either don't believe in it or don't recognize it, we just slough it off or dismiss it completely. I don't pretend to understand it fully, but I do know it exists.

In this book I will share with you the things I have experienced and what I have learned about the interaction of that "other realm" with our present existence. Some have been great encounters and others not so great, but nevertheless, they have all been interesting and educational. It has only been through the recent experiences after the death of my beloved, sweet, wonderful husband, Paul Hayford, that it has become clearer that the "veil" is *very* thin. This has caused me to look back over my life and realize how often that veil has been crossed–I never fully understood it until now.

My hope is that in some way your faith in our wonderful, loving Heavenly Father will increase and help you realize how much He is watching over us in so many different ways. As Jeremiah 29:11 states, "'For I know the plans I have for you,' declares the Lord, 'plans to prosper you and not to harm you, plans to give you hope and a future.'" It was no accident that we were born, for He formed each one of us in the womb and planned us even before that (Isaiah 44:2, 49:1, Jeremiah 1:5), each one of us uniquely equipped to fulfill a specific purpose on this earth in the Body of Christ. He created us to do a specific job, at a specific time in history, and placed us in the family that would shape and train us to fulfill that purpose. It may be hard to believe that because you had a very tough upbringing. It is never God's will for anyone to suffer, but if you will give Him a chance to love you and heal you of those hurts, he has promised in Romans 8:28, "And we know that in all things God works for the good of those who love Him, who have been called according to his purpose." He will make something good come of all your pain and suffering. As you triumph over your trials and tribulations, you become better able to help others who are going through the same things. II Corinthians 1:3-4, "Praise be to the God and Father of our Lord Jesus Christ, the

Father of compassion and the God of all comfort, who comforts us in all our troubles so that we can comfort those in any trouble with the comfort we ourselves have received from God."You need to "Cast all your anxiety on Him for He cares for us" (I Peter 5:7). He has promised He will never leave us nor forsake us in Hebrews 13:5-6. In John 14, especially verses 1-3 and 26, He promised the Holy Spirit to be with us, teach us, lead us and comfort us. So many times in my life I had felt that God left me, as though I was calling out to a blank wall, "where are you?" But in looking back over my life, I can see how the hand of God orchestrated circumstances to preserve His will for me. Perhaps I was born for this day and time in history. Just as Queen Esther in Esther 4:14 was chosen for her day, so are each one of us. I don't know fully why or what His complete plan is for me, all I know is that He has been there all my life, holding my hand and never giving up when I disobeyed or strayed. He has brought me comfort in ways I could never imagine (some of those miraculous instances are illustrated in this book) and I am assured He will continue doing the same until I step into His presence. I know that I belong to Him, I love Him with all my heart, soul, and spirit and that the Holy Spirit is guiding me: His angels are watching over me and I could never be in a safer place than when I am walking with Him. I pray that this book will help you understand how the enemy of our soul, Satan, seeks to destroy and steal all that God has planned for us. We are warned in I Peter 5:8 to "Be self-controlled and alert. Your enemy the devil, prowls around like a roaring lion, looking for someone to devour." He is constantly looking for ways to "devour" God's wonderful plan for us and get us distracted or even killed in order to thwart that plan. BUT GOD won't let that happen if you will commit your life to Him. If you don't think Satan exists, just look around you. Evil, chaos, deceit and immorality are everywhere. Just remember, "You dear children are from God and have overcome them, because the One who is in you is greater than the one who is in the World (I John 4:4)."

In some ways, perhaps, what I have to share will be educational as well as fun to read. Welcome to my journey as I relate what I have heard, seen, and experienced as I walked the Thin Veil between the "Seen and Unseen."

# CHAPTER 1

# FIRST ENCOUNTERS

*I* was definitely not wanted. I can't blame my mother for feeling that way because she was 45 years old when she discovered she was three months pregnant with me. She had already borne 7 children and raised her brother's daughter after he was killed in an automobile accident. My brothers and sisters told me about her disappointment, but because my mother didn't believe in abortion, she endured the pregnancy in great sorrow. I was born in the warm month of July, 1938, in Long Island, New York, and all seemed to go well until winter hit. I am sure God had a definite purpose for me in His mind. Satan knew it and wanted to thwart that purpose by trying to kill me in January 1939 when I developed pneumonia and nearly died. Doctors didn't have the antibiotics we have today to combat that horrible disease, so all they could do was apply poultices to my tiny chest, wrap me in warm blankets, put me in a room with the windows wide open, and pray that the cold air would help my lungs so I could breathe. No one expected me to live. But God had other plans and since He is greater than Satan, He touched my tiny body and I gradually recovered.

Life was pretty normal for the next 13 years as we moved to a farm in upstate New York. Dad was a city boy, so as my brothers grew and left home, the farm was just too much for him to handle alone. He finally sold it and moved to the city of Hudson Falls, New York. We lived there for about four years before we finally moved to North Argyle, a very small community about 10 miles East of Hudson Falls/Ft. Edward, where my mother got the dream house of her life, and I experienced my first encounter with a spirit that crossed the Thin Veil into my life.*

Mom had a favorite poem which always hung on our wall called the "House by the Side of the Road." Why she loved it and dreamed of having a house by the side of the road she never said, but here it is.

Let me live in a house by the side of the road,
Where the race of men go by—
The men who are good and the men who are bad,
As good and as bad as I.
I would not sit in the scorner's seat
Or hurl the cynic's ban—
Let me live in a house by the side of the road
And be a friend to man.

Mom got her house by the side of the road, but unfortunately it was her last one on this earth. No one had ever revealed the fact that every family previous to our moving in had had one member of their family die there. Years later, in checking back with the current owners, I learned that my mother was the last one to die in that house and no one has ever experienced any of the phenomena that had plagued us. Let me tell you about them.

Next to our house there was an old, huge, rundown two-story mansion, with ancient-looking drapes covering the windows. We knew someone occupied it, but in all the two years we lived there, we never saw anyone coming or going. I still don't know who resided in that house. It looked soooo old and kind of run down. I would often sit in my upstairs bedroom window which faced that house and look for someone, anyone to appear, but no one ever did. Our bathroom was off the kitchen on the ground floor facing the back field. One night I was soaking in the tub, singing and enjoying myself, when I looked up at the window and saw a man's face watching me. I remember screaming my head off and wouldn't get out of the tub to unlock the door until he disappeared. My dad rushed out the back door as soon as I told him what happened, but all he could find were foot and hand prints in the mud, leading through the barb wire fence and over toward that house next door. There was a large field between us that was muddy near our house, but the ground further away became hard. That was where the footsteps stopped. We never knew if the peeping tom was someone from that house or someone walking down the road. We were way out in the country so the likelihood of someone walking by and climbing the barb wire fence, in the mud, to peek in a back window, is pretty low. Since we never saw anyone next door, we had no idea if a man lived there or not. I never saw that face again. Strange!!

For years that peeping tom left a scar on my emotions. Amazing how one little shock like that can affect you for so long. I was terrified of looking up in a window at night and seeing someone watching me. I kept the curtains closed to hide the windows, but no one that I ever saw showed up. The only other incident that reminded me of that night was when I was in my 20's, living alone with my three German Shepherds in El Monte, California. I am a night owl and one night I started receiving obscene phone calls. I just brushed it off until my three German Shepherds became agitated. I opened the back door to let them out and saw the reason why. I have never seen anyone clear a fence as fast as that backyard intruder when he saw my snarling pack of dogs rushing towards him. I never saw him near my window because my curtains were shut, but the dogs knew he was there. Gradually over time that phobia left me, but back to the House by the Side of the Road story.

The "ghost" in the house in North Argyle was my first real encounter with a non-physical being. There was an empty attic off my bedroom that was never used. I checked that room many times and never found a trace of anything but dust, yet that attic had some kind of spirit presence. Every night I would push a big dresser up against the door and pile a big, old 9 x 12 carpet on top of it. It was on a hardwood floor, so moving that dresser was quite noisy, to say the least. Every morning, without fail, the dresser was pushed back to its original position along with the rug, and the attic door was wide open, not a crack, but w-i-d-e open. I never felt or heard anything, but it was moved. I wasn't the only one who knew it, because when I had friends sleep over, they witnessed the same phenomena. Needless to say, they refused to stay again. Every night I would hunker down, hiding under the covers head and all, and went to sleep as fast as I could. I knew that whatever it was, entered my room, passed over me in bed (I could sense the presence but didn't see anything) and did whatever it did to move those things, but never awakened me from sleep or made a sound. I didn't like it, but never really felt afraid of it, and it never touched or harmed me. It continued as long as we lived there, which was only a few months after my mother's death.

In those days, we didn't have light switches, just strings that hung down from the second floor ceiling light to the bottom of the stairs so we could pull the strings and turn the light on, thus making it possible for us to see as we ascended the stairs and walked down the hallway between the two bedrooms. My mother died in her downstairs bedroom at 2:30 in the morning. We never thought anything about what started to happen because nothing had ever happened before, not even when she was laid out in the room below my bedroom as was the custom for wakes and funerals in those days. It started after she was laid to rest in the cemetery nearby. At 2:30 every morning we heard someone or something start ascending the stairs, beginning about the 5th step up, climb 5 steps and fade out. It sounded like a person shuffling up the old, creaking wooden steps. My sister, Florence, who had the other bedroom on the second floor, also heard it. We would often stand at the top of the stairs with our hands on the light chain and wait. As soon as we heard, whatever it was, take two steps, we pulled the light chain only to find out nothing was there. As soon as we made a sound or the light came on, the steps stopped. We tried having people stand at the bottom of the stairs and at the top; everyone heard it, but no one ever saw anything.

I am an avid swimmer, taught swimming, worked as a lifeguard, swam in a water ballet group and felt like a fish in the water. The water was my friend and I never felt afraid in it, not even as a very young woman. I would stay in the water until I looked like a dried burnt prune. The only way my family got me out of the lake to go home, was to literally drag me out of the water. One day, when I was about 9 years old, I was at the lake with a group of kids from school. One of the girls who couldn't swim was playing out on the dock. Something happened and she fell in. The other kids were all screaming and no one would go in to pull her out of the bottom of the lake where she was lying, drowning. I remember seeing her, but don't remember diving in and pulling her out. When I was at a class reunion years later, my former classmates reminded me of the incident, but all I remember is seeing her there and that I had no fear of the water.

Being from upper state New York, we only swam in lakes and rivers. I never had any experience with ocean currents and tides and was unaware that receding tides can take things out to sea. We moved to Sarasota, Florida, across the street from the Gulf of Mexico where my younger sister Yvonne and I spent nearly every afternoon after school playing on the beach. I had a habit of floating on the water and falling asleep, lulled by the warm sun and the gentle rocking of the waves. I didn't know it was a dangerous thing to do. One afternoon I must have been asleep for at least an hour because when I woke up, I tried to stand. There was no bottom and I could barely see the shoreline. I started to panic. All I could think of was that my stepmom was going to kill me because I was supposed to be watching my little sister. I started swimming as rapidly as I could for shore. Unfortunately, I had never swum in waves before and with every few strokes, a wave would knock me under and I would swim all the more frantically. I had only been struggling for a few seconds when a man appeared beside me and talked me into quieting down. What are the chances that a mere, mortal man would have been swimming close to me that far out in the Gulf of Mexico? He told me how to swim with the waves instead of fighting them. All I could think about was my little sister, to which he replied, "I can see her playing on the beach, and she is fine." I only took a few strokes when, without any feeling of movement, I was *instantly* at the shore, standing up and walking out of the water. I turned to thank the man who had helped me, but he had vanished. There was no way he could have swam or walked away that fast as Siesta Key beach was wide open and stretched for over ½-mile with a clear, unobstructed view. I didn't think anything about what had happened until years later when I realized it had to be an angel, for who else could have appeared next to me at least a half mile out in the gulf, instantly get me to shore with no feeling of movement, and then vanish from sight faster than I could glance around to see my sister sitting there and look back to find him gone. If he was a mortal man, at the most, he would have only been able to take about 5 steps on that beach before I would have turned around to thank him. Only an angel could vanish that fast on that open beach.

On my 16th birthday, my Dad taught me to drive and helped me get my license. I had only been driving for a few months when tragedy struck. My step brother in New York was involved in an automobile accident that was so bad they didn't expect him to live. Since we couldn't afford the plane tickets for all of us, Mom flew to New York to be by his side, while Dad, Yvonne and I drove north. We didn't have freeways in those days so two-lane highways were common routes to take. Late one evening, dad became so tired he decided to let me drive while he napped in the back seat. A few hours later, as I was going around a sharp curve, the right front tire suddenly blew out pulling the car to the right and heading off the road. I felt a force grab the steering wheel and pull the car back on the road. I sat there with my hands loosely on the wheel, feeling it turn left under the "angel's power." I never touched the brake or applied any pressure to the wheel, but the car came to a safe halt. How they do that I don't know, but as quickly as I felt it come over me, felt the power of that wheel turn, and watched the brake go to the floor and stop us, it was gone. I don't know how they can cross that Veil and do what they do to the physical world when they are obviously in an invisible form. It blows my mind. God definitely had a plan for my life and no matter how Satan tried to kill me, He wasn't about to let that happen.

# CHAPTER 2

# NEW DIRECTIONS

After high school, I entered Columbia Bible College (nka, Columbia International University) in Columbia, South Carolina, to learn how to work with orphaned children in Cuba. I had the wonderful privilege of visiting that Island with its warm, friendly people at the end of my junior year and fell in love with the children at the orphanage. I loved everything about the culture, the people, the terrain, and especially the food. I couldn't wait to get back there after graduation only to have my hopes crushed when Castro took over and closed the door to any Christian involvement from outside the Island. I was heartbroken, but believed that God had something else in mind or another place He had chosen for me. I started to apply to several mission boards that focused on work with children in other countries, preferably in Spanish speaking countries as I loved the language and the Spanish people.

With every application, I was turned down for the same reason, I was too strong a person and too independent to serve as one of their missionaries. They felt that I would think outside the box, and not listen to their instructions or obey their guidelines. Looking back now, I can see that God gave me that personality because He had other plans for me, but at the time, I became greatly discouraged. I wanted to serve the Lord and Him only by helping orphaned children. I just couldn't understand what was wrong.

Then life changed drastically. I moved back to Sarasota, Florida, with my parents and tried to figure out what I was going to do with a Bachelor of Biblical Education. I could serve in the Church, which I did, but I kept seeking God's overall plan for my life. That is when Satan threw in an obstacle, a trial in the form of a man, to distract me from God's overall plan. I was living with my voice teacher, trading care of her for lessons, and earned extra money as a soloist at the Jewish Temple where my teacher worked as the organist. Things were okay and life was uneventful until I met Frank Klein, a friend of my voice teacher. He had come to the house to visit, and it was nearly love at first sight. He was so gallant, asking my teacher if he could date me, showering me with attention, and making me feel very special. He started attending church with me and even professed Christ as His Savior. When he asked me to marry him, I fully trusted him and said yes. This was the biggest mistake of my life because I didn't ask God if this was <u>His</u> choice for me, just went on my own female emotions. Satan sure knew what buttons to push in my life to get me off track from God's plan. I am so thankful the Lord doesn't give up on us when we stray, but as Romans 8:28 says, "And we know that God causes all things to work together for good to those who love God, to those who are called according to His purpose." As you will see, He did just that in spite of the fact that there were consequences to pay in the meantime.

Things were a bit rocky, but in 1962, we went ahead with the wedding. That was when Frank changed. There was another whole side of him I had never seen and when the abuse started, life became hell. I realized then that I had made a terrible mistake, but since I didn't believe in divorce, I stuck it out, on and off, for 8 years. We separated several times, but I believed him when he said he had changed and I went back for another try. During one of those many reconciliations we moved to El Monte, California. In that little house is where my experiences with the Thin Veil came to the forefront, becoming more and more a part of my life. One day, an Avon lady came by to sell me some perfume. We started talking and soon got around to spiritual things. When she asked me if I had received the Baptism of the Holy Spirit, I told her I had never heard of such a need. As a Baptist, I had been taught that speaking in tongues and miracles all died with the Disciples, and all the gifts they experienced ended with them. During my Bible College days, a friend and I decided we would see what Pentecostals were all about, so one Sunday we attended a "holy roller" church where everyone was running around, rolling on the floor and jabbering what sounded like gibberish. We got out of there as fast as we could and never looked back. These actions are what I equated with the Baptism of the Holy Spirit. I didn't think I needed any additional Baptism because I already had the Holy Spirit as a seal of my salvation, as is expressed in Ephesians 1:13, "In whom we also trusted, after you heard the word of truth, the gospel of your salvation; in whom also after you believed, you were sealed with that Holy Spirit of promise."

Soon after the Avon lady's visit, I was reading a book by Roy Rogers and Dale Evans in which they talked about receiving the Baptism of the Holy Spirit. It piqued my interest as they seemed to be such normal people. I had visited their church in Apple Valley where I had the privilege of meeting them and found them to be kind, sweet, shy but gentle people who deeply loved and honored God. They weren't acting crazy, but normal like anyone else, even the service was quiet and in order. About that time, Stuart Hamblen wrote the song, "It is no secret what God can do, what He's done for others He'll do for you. With arms wide open He'll pardon you, it is no secret what God can do." Slowly it began to dawn on me that in God's eyes, I was no different from Roy and Dale or anyone else who had surrendered their lives to Christ, all I had to do was sur- render my total being to God for Him to do with as He willed. I decided that whatever it was, I wanted all God had for me, not missing a thing. I'm kind of greedy that way. I realized that the Baptism wasn't receiving the Holy Spirit, but was in reality opening up my life to the in-filling and control of the Holy Spirit, holding nothing back. I wanted it all no matter what the cost. One day, I knelt by my bed and opened every door of my being to the in-filling and control of the Holy Spirit, including my tongue. I quietly started to sing to the Lord. After many minutes of worship, I realized I was singing in a language I didn't know. From that time on, I would often pray in the Spirit when praying for someone's needs. We can't know the inward workings and desires of someone else, but the Holy Spirit knows them. When we ask Him to pray through us, He is able to pray perfectly for every situation. The Holy Spirit prayed for them through me in a way I couldn't.

This new relationship with the Holy Spirit began to open new doors for me. For awhile I wasn't certain if I was speaking gibberish (like the Pentecostals I had once accused), I didn't understand a word of what I was saying. That mystery was cleared up when one day a lady from Egypt asked me to pray for her migraine headache. I laid hands on her and when I started to pray, God told me to pray in tongues. I had never done that in public before, but I did it in this situation out of obedience. When I finished praying she looked at me with the biggest eyes of wonderment that I had ever seen and said, "Where did you learn perfect Coptic Hebrew?" I replied, "I didn't learn it, I don't know a word of Hebrew except for the prayers I'd learn to sing in the Jewish Temple. Why do you ask?" She then told me that she and her husband had escaped Egypt because they were Orthodox Jews and I had prayed for her in perfect Coptic Hebrew. From that day on, I never again doubted the validity of praying in tongues. I love I Corinthians 14, because it gives clear, specific instructions as to how, why, and when we are to pray in tongues, specifically verses 39, 40, which say, "Therefore, my brothers, be eager to prophesy, and do not forbid speaking in tongues. But everything should be done in a fitting and orderly way."

While all of this was happening, Frank bought me a beautiful German shepherd puppy we named Princessa. Oh, how I loved that dog and my how she loved children. We lived next to an apartment building that had lots of them in residence. Every morning they would knock on my door and ask if Princessa could come out and play. She couldn't get out the door fast enough to be with them. I knew exactly when the kids went in, because she would come home, open the back door by pulling on a toy I had attached to it, and plop down on the couch, totally worn out. The parents would tell me how much they appreciated that dog because they never had to worry about the kids when she was around. She wouldn't let any stranger near her precious charges. They were safe with her and everyone knew it.

The days were filled with great times with her – she became my friend, my true companion, my comforter and crying pillow. One day, when she was about a year old, I was working in the kitchen and I heard a terrible noise in the bedroom. I ran in to find Princessa having a violent seizure. I held her until it was over. The vet couldn't find anything wrong with her and sent us home to see if anything changed. The second seizure occurred about three months later; the third one, two months after that; then, another seizure a month later, until one day she started seizing and couldn't stop. We rushed her to the vet, who gave her heavy medication to stop them. We left her overnight so the vet could monitor her only to receive his call in the morning to inform us that she had died during the night. She had a brain tumor that grew so large it crushed her brain to where life for her was unsustainable. On a dog, brain surgery was not possible, so she left me.

I was inconsolable. I had known grief before, but never like this. In the misery of my life and marriage, she had been the only light I had and now that too was gone. A few days later, I was sitting on the edge of my bed, weeping with sobs that tore to the center of my being. I looked up and to my surprise, Princessa was sitting in front of me. I was in shock. Suddenly, with no sign or feeling of movement, just as I had experienced in my rescue on the beach, she was in my arms and I was holding her for dear life. I will never forget the feeling of holding her once again in my arms until, without sign of or feeling of movement, she was sitting in front of me again. Looking up at me she clearly said, "I was <u>allowed to come back and tell you I am okay and that I will see you when you get here</u>." I remember begging her to stay, but she said she had to go back and vanished. Oh how thin that veil is and how quickly and easily they seem to pass back and forth through it. I know that because I know Christ as My Savior, my sins have been forgiven and as Jesus promised in John

14:1-4, He will come again to get us and take us there, that I will be reunited with my beloved pets. I will never doubt that again. This was the beginning of my mind opening to more and more of the reality of how thin the veil between the seen and unseen really is.

Months later, I was still grieving, so Frank sent me home to visit my parents in the hopes that it would get me through this rough time. I was lying on my old bed, crying one day, when all of a sudden the ceiling opened up and that thin veil was pulled back so I could see in. There she was playing in the most beautiful, clean, living forest. She ran into the stream to retrieve a rock, which she often did on our walks in the hills above Azusa. The thing that impressed me was how pretty she looked and when she dove for rocks, they were all smooth and beautiful, not like the ones in the streams we traversed on our walks. As she exited the water, her coat was full and dry–in the water, but never really wet. So different from when she would come out of the stream on our walks when her coat was always a gnarled mess that took hours to dry. I watched her for several minutes until she trotted over to the edge of the vision, looked down at me and said, "I'll see you when you get here." The vision ended and so did my deep sorrow. I will always miss seeing her here on earth, but I know what it looks like where she is "living now" and it is beautiful; most of all, she is happy. I know that I am going there and I know beyond any shadow of a doubt that my beloved animals are enjoying themselves while they wait for me. Little did I know what God was about to do, and how he used all of this to open my eyes to His perfect will for me.

Life began to get very interesting from that point on as I learned to listen to the Holy Spirit. I attended a small interdenominational, Spirit-filled, prayer group at the local Episcopal Church led by Father Harriott. One evening, someone came to me and said, "God told me to give you this book. There is something in there He wants to teach you. The book was by J. Allen Boone called, "Kinship with All Life," where he talks about his experience of communicating with his dog Strongheart and other animals. I thought it was pretty interesting, but didn't really think anything of it until another person in the group, totally unrelated to the person who gave me the book, approached me with a pamphlet about understanding the human subconscious mind. Wow, I was beginning to see a pattern. I asked the Holy Spirit what it was He wanted me to learn.

It wasn't long after I read these materials that things really started happening. As I was walking down the street one day, I felt someone calling me, only to discover that a dog was standing behind the fence staring at me. The communication was so clear, I knew it was real. I checked out his story when I met the owners, and the dog was right. A guard dog across the street was also staring intently at me so I walked over to pet him. He told me he was lonely and really needed some love. I later learned that NO ONE had ever been able to touch that dog while he was on duty guarding the business. I was stunned but decided I would try a couple of Boone's experiments. I had two situations in my back yard that were perplexing to me. They both had to do with a magnificent plum tree that yielded so much fruit, I could give baskets full to the poor children in the neighborhood. The only trouble was that the birds would land in the tree, eat a little bit of each plum and leave the rest. Between them destroying the fruit and making it inedible for people, the termites were eating the tree from the inside. I decided to see if they would respond if I "talked" to them, so I stood under the tree and said, first to the termites, "If you will leave my backyard and the trees here, I will not kill you. There is an old log in the field out back so you can have it, but if you insist on staying in my yard and trees, I will have to kill you." Then I addressed the birds, "If you will leave the fruit alone, every plum that falls off the tree, I will leave for you to feast on. But if you insist on destroying the fruit, I will have to do something to harm you and make you stay away." To my amazement, the next day I noticed the termites were gone, but later discovered them in the old log out in the field. That year, the birds NEVER touched the fruit on the tree but ate heartily from the ones on the ground. Wow, this really worked, but what was I supposed to do with what I was learning? These stories and what grew out of them are related in my books, "What the Animals Tell Me" and "Stories the Animals Tell Me," now revised and added to my most recent book, "You Too Can Talk with the Animals." This was a whole new realm of how the Lord was leading me to cross the Thin Veil between man and animals. What an exciting adventure, and a new way of living was mine to enjoy. I thought everyone would understand for God had led me. I began to hear His voice the same way I heard the animal's voices, like thoughts that just came into my head clearly and unmistakably from Him. I always made sure that I checked out everything I heard with the Bible as I knew God would never give me anything contrary to His word. I loved fellowshipping with Him as new life poured into my being.

One evening, I attended a revival service at a Pentecostal church in Pasadena. The preacher was dynamic as he expounded the Word of God and later ministered to individuals in the congregation. He was known to be a great man of God among the evangelicals. You can imagine my surprise when he walked up to me, pointed his finger in my face and said, "You are from Satan spreading his evil lies about talking to animals. That is evil." I was stunned and speechless. I fled from that service to get on my face before God to find out what went wrong. I felt He was leading me all the way, and here a man of God pointed me out as evil? Who am I to question such a great man who walked with and served God? I told God that I would never pick it up again if it was evil; I only wanted to serve Him and not do anything that would dishonor Him. I needed Him to show me, once and for all, exactly what this was all about. As hard as it would be, I told Him I would lay it down and never do it again if that preacher was right. I was devastated to think I had been dishonoring to my wonderful Heavenly Father.

I began to search the Scriptures, looking for anything God had to say about the animals. Starting in Genesis, I discovered that for Adam and Eve it was apparently common for them to talk with the animals. Why else do you think Eve conversed with the serpent as one would talk with another intelligent being and respond in a way that showed she believed the serpent? If it wasn't common to chat with animals, then don't you think her reaction would have been different? This reminds me of an ad on TV that I love. It is a little boy sitting in a carriage when a mime comes up and talks to his mother and the insurance salesman. When the mime leaves, the little boy says, "Does anyone else think it is strange that the mime is talking? Freeeeeeky!" If that had been the first time Eve had talked WITH an animal, I imagine she would have reacted differently, maybe even finding it "freeeeeeky!" Until this happened, the serpent had been a beautiful creature that walked on legs, but God punished it by taking its legs away and condemned it to slither on the ground and eat dust because it had allowed Satan to use it to cause man to sin.

How about Noah? If there wasn't a relationship between man and animals, how do you think they willingly entered the ark? He didn't go out and lasso them and drag them in (try that with a lion or badger and see how far you get), but they came willingly, prompted by God, I am sure, and lived peacefully together in the ark with Noah. That is one amazing scene I would love to have witnessed. I wonder if God will replay it on some kind of screen when we get there. You get a taste of it from the Movie "Noah" although little else in the film was accurate. I believe, and this is just Lydecker-Hayford theology, that when they came off the ark, that relationship was broken as God allotted them to man as food and put the fear of man in them (Genesis 9:1-9). The loss of that special bond between man and animals was broken, but it didn't negate the thinking capacity of the animals nor does it give us license to abuse them as Proverbs 12:10 states, "A righteous man cares for the needs of his animals, but the kindest acts of the wicked, are cruel." This is further exemplified in Numbers 22:21-35, the

Ass saw the angel, but until God opened her mouth to speak to Balaam in a way he could understand (was it literally verbal like Mr. Ed on TV, or was it the way they speak to me, through the mind?), Balaam didn't know there was a problem. God then removed the Thin Veil and allowed Balaam to "see" the angel standing in the way and conversed with him. I have learned from many of my animal clients that the veil doesn't seem to be there for them, only for us. They easily see beings we can't. I will tell you some of those stories later. This is just one example of how the animals have suffered at the selfishness and rage of man, mostly because they can't understand what is going on in the animal's mind and why they do what they do. However, the sin of man affects all of creation not just the serpent, as explained in Romans 8:22 and 23 that says, "We know that the whole creation has been groaning as right up to the present time. Not only so, but we ourselves, who have the first fruits of the Spirit, groan inwardly as we wait eagerly for our adoption as sons, the redemption of our bodies." This is talking about the second coming of Christ when we shall all be taken up into heaven where we will no longer feel pain or sorrow, worry or fear.

I found another passage in Ecclesiastes 3:21, a book that is talking about life as man sees it, from man's perspective, not God's. The writer is questioning, "Who knows if the spirit of man rises upward and if the spirit of the animal goes down into the earth?" I knew from experience that animals did have a soul that lived after they died, as did man, and a spirit that could feel all the emotions we feel. They also think somewhat like us, but are limited in their ability to make plans and understand complicated concepts. Only man had that part of him that was "in the image of God," and that part was marred in the fall of Adam; because we can and do sin, Christ had to die as our atonement. The animals don't need forgiveness: they are totally aware of their Creator; it is only man who needs a Savior. I have NEVER FOUND ANYTHING IN THE BIBLE THAT SAYS WHAT ADAM AND EVE ENJOYED WITH THE ANIMALS, STOPPED WHEN THEY LEFT THE GARDEN.

I asked God why He called me to talk with the animals, and how to experience the Thin Veil between this world and the supernatural, and he brought me an answer. A few days after the preacher condemned me, I received a call from a client whose dog I had chatted with. I remembered her telling me how she had started delving into the occult because she loved her animals and knew there was more to them than what appeared on the surface. The New Agers knew it too and were capitalizing on that to pull people into their philosophies. We had talked about her relationship with these groups and how that was not pleasing to God who truly cared about her and her animals. My conversation with her animals made that crystal clear. She had called to thank me for helping her realize where she was headed by attending their meetings and now she had turned back to the Lord, recommitting her life to Him.

As I was praying at church about what had happened, and the follow-up phone call from my client, I heard God tell me why He let that preacher condemn me. "Satan has had my truth long enough. I want my people to know what I have for them with the animals, but most of all, I want you to listen only to me. Never again are you to doubt what I tell you to do no matter what man says. I, and I only, am your God. You will face much criticism from the world and from Christians, but you are to stand firm and do what I tell you to do. Never waiver from my calling. If you are faithful to my calling, I will justify you." Oh, how true that became as I talked more and more openly about my work with animal communication. It seemed for awhile like the whole world thought I was a joke as they poked fun at me and Christians condemned me. It was hard to take, but I would never again doubt my Lord. He told me to do as He said and someday He would justify me. He has definitely fulfilled that promise. The Holy Spirit also reminded me that Isaiah 54:17 states, "No weapon that is forged against you shall prevail, and you will refute every tongue that accuses you. This is the heritage of the servants of the Lord, and this is their vindication from me." Romans 11:29 says, "For God's gifts and His call are irrevocable." I believe there are all kinds of gifts God wants to bestow on people, but they never experience them because they are afraid to trust God and step out in faith, they are afraid to be different. When someone comes to me now and informs me that God told them I was wrong in what I do, my answer now is this: You better check the source of your information, because God told me differently and I choose to believe the Holy Spirit over your source. God doesn't speak with a forked tongue, telling me one thing and you another. I know who my source is, you better check yours.

When things settled down and I grew in the Spirit, little did I know that I was about to experience the Hand of God in an even more miraculous way. I once had a lovely neighbor who also loved the Lord and her children. Her name was Mel and her husband's name was George. He was a bona fide alcoholic who stopped to get drunk every night on his way home from work. He then spent his evenings abusing his family who were terrified of him. One day, I was sitting in my living room when I heard God say to me, "Get over there now, George is going to kill his family." I had never interfered before, but this time without even a second of hesitation, I tore out my back door, across the driveway and opened their back door. I yelled, "In the name of Jesus, George, you leave your family alone." He stormed to the back door carrying a metal pipe that he had been using on his family. He raised that pipe and prepared to swing at my head when suddenly he couldn't move his arm. It was suspended in the air, and no matter how hard he tried to swing it or bring it down, he couldn't. He grabbed his arm with his other hand and pulled with all his might, but it was obvious someone was holding that arm back. I yelled for Mel and Lisa to get over to my house immediately. As I heard my front door slam shut, knowing they were safe, I slowly started to back up. When I got across the drive and near my door, his hand holding the pipe dropped like a rock. He had the most terrified look on his face and from that day on, if he saw me anywhere, he would cross the road to get away from me. Little did he know that an angel was holding that arm, I had nothing to do with it. This time an angel had crossed the Thin Veil: He was felt, but not seen. Without the prompting of God, I would never have done what I did, but I knew God told me to, so all I am required to do is obey. It is up to God to handle the consequences. That experience helped me understand what I read about the Six-Day War in Israel in 1967. Many of the Israeli troops would approach an enemy vehicle full of soldiers with an arsenal of guns that far outnumbered the Jewish army, and aimed right at the Israelis. But instead of firing at the Israeli troops, the enemy just sat there until they were totally captured. When asked why they didn't shoot their guns, they replied, "We couldn't. Our arms became paralyzed." I know firsthand how

God's army of angels can do that. I saw the same thing in this incident with George. As God promised, He protected His people, just as He promises to take care of us. Wow, what a God we serve. I'm sure glad I'm on His side. Ephesians 6 tells us that we wrestle not against flesh and blood, but against principalities and powers. Because of what was happening to me, that scripture became real. Romans 8:31 also tells us that "...if God is for us, who can be against us?" That became more and more obvious every day.

It wasn't long before I again experienced, but couldn't see, the Hand of God. If you have ever been to Los Angeles during rush hour you will definitely understand the story I am about to tell. I was driving along the middle lane of the 10 freeway, heading home for El Monte. The traffic was flowing slowly, but steadily, until we got just below Temple City. Suddenly, everything became chaos. Cars were hitting each other like a train wreck in the very lane I was in. All lanes on both sides of me were full and cars were coming behind me at such a fast speed there was no way I could avoid being rear-ended and pushed into the car in front of me. It was a horrible situation I could not avoid. All I could do was cry out to God, "Jesus, Jesus, Jesus." Suddenly, without feeling movement or anything, just like when the angel saved my life and brought me to shore, I was instantly in the outside lane passing the pileup. I was stunned, but so grateful God sent His angels to once again get me out of a bad situation and save my life.

In looking back over Psalm 91, I can sure see the Hand of the Lord who has sent His angels to watch over me. That Psalm reflects my desire to serve Him and Him only in my life. Unfortunately, like David, I have disobeyed and done some pretty stupid and even sinful things, but God knows my heart and has rescued me every time.

# CHAPTER 3

# SINGLE AGAIN

The next encounter happened around 1972 while living on a small farm in the Bradbury Estates as caretakers for an absentee owner. It was a fun place in many ways, the dogs had great freedom to roam the several acres, and we had chickens for our own fresh eggs and lots of Avocados from the small grove on the property. The dogs loved them too, developing beautiful shiny coats as they snacked on the ones they found in the leaves that had ripened and fallen to the ground. One of the cow pastures backed up to some houses where a lot of children lived. They would visit us often following me around while I gathered eggs. It sure gave me a chuckle when the kids would ask me why I stored my eggs in the chicken house. They had only seen their parents pick them up at the store and didn't realize they came from chickens.

I had one chicken that was determined to roost on a piece of farm equipment in the open barn. Every night I had to retrieve her and put her in the hen house to protect her from the many coyotes lurking around for dinner. One night, I found her sitting on the mower handle and reached for her, but a soft voice said, "Check your next move." I looked around but didn't see anyone so reached for her again. The voice was not so soft anymore as it said, "Check your next move." I couldn't see any reason for it so ignored the second time only to have "it" nearly shout at me, "Check your next move!" About that time, I figured I'd better listen and went inside for a flashlight. When I came out again, I shined that light everywhere but no one was around. As I shined the light on the chicken, I saw why that voice from the other side of the Veil stopped me. Right above the hen, there was a new spider web with a black widow spider sitting in the middle of it waiting for dinner to arrive. Had I ignored the voice, I would have grabbed that spider before I reached the chicken and only God knew what was going to happen. They are bountiful in Southern California and can be quite deadly. Once again, someone had crossed that Thin Veil and saved my life. I was sure grateful whoever or whatever it was didn't give up warning me until I listened. Never felt or saw anything, just a voice that this time was audible.

Things had pretty much come to a head in my marriage. We started going to Narramore Christian Counseling Center to see if we could make it work, but all my husband would do is tell the counselor he was paying for the sessions to make me do what he wanted. I kept going by myself for awhile because I wanted to find out why I had married this man in the first place, hoping I wouldn't make the same mistake again. People usually do marry the same kind of person they divorce, so I worked hard to avoid that pitfall and change my focus. The last straw was the day my husband went crazy, chased me into the field with a strand of barb wire and tried to strangle me with it. The next day I packed my personal things and left for good. I felt that I could be a better witness for God as a live divorcée than a dead wife. It was one of the hardest things I ever did because I felt I was letting God down. I had no job except for the few consultations I did with animals, no money and no solid means of support. I knew that I was going to have to rely on God to take care of me.

I bounced from one church to another because when they found out I was divorced, they would no longer let me sing in the choir or participate in any of their functions. Oh, I could attend, but you might as well have sewn a scarlet letter "D" on my chest. As far as they were concerned, I had committed the unpardonable sin of getting a divorce, and I was an outcast. The first Assembly of God in North Hollywood accepted me, but when they found out I talked to animals, they branded me as occultist. Finally, about 1973, I found my way home to Church on The Way. Jack Hayford, and eventually his son-in-law, Scott Bauer, welcomed me with open arms. They understood my heart for the Lord and never judged me for what had happened, but continued to encourage me to keep doing what the Lord had called me to do. That church became my lifeline for the next 24 years where I soaked up the Word every chance I could. Jack Hayford's and Scott Bauer's teachings were exactly what this hungry soul needed.

I remember one meeting with hundreds of people in attendance, that surprised me quit a bit. I was still new in walking the Thin Veil with the Holy Spirit, so what was about to happen was a bit unsettling. The front filled up fast as everyone wanted to be close to the podium, but I finally found a couple of vacant seats about half way back. This left only two seats in that section open which were soon occupied by a young couple, the woman sat quietly beside me. While we were all standing, singing those wonderful songs that were mostly written by Jack Hayford, God spoke to me. "I want you to sit down and put your arm around the woman sitting next to you and tell her that the child she so longs to hold in her arms will be hers one day soon." I stopped singing long enough to argue with God. I was so afraid of being wrong and embarrassed; I knew I'd never live it down. "You are kidding, right? You want me to tell her she will soon have the baby she wants? I don't even know her!" "Yes," He responded. "I know her and that is all that is needed. All you are required to do is obey, the rest is up to me." One thing I was learning, was not to question God when He tells you something, no matter what it feels like. You can imagine how I felt as with trepidation, I sat down, placed my arm around her shoulder and whispered God's message to her. She started to sob as she told me that that very day, she had miscarried her baby that she so desperately wanted. What a relief as I became aware that the message for her was right on target. I saw them again about a year later. I didn't remember what she looked like, but she remembered me. With a big grin that went from ear to ear, she held up her precious bundle (I think it was a boy, but don't remember for sure) who was going to be dedicated that day. "Look," she said, "He did it!" I was so glad I had obeyed. It was one more reassurance that the voice I was hearing was that of the Holy Spirit.

About this time, someone brought me a copy of a book by Ruth Carter Stapleton, sister of Jimmy Carter, married to Dr. Stapleton, a veterinarian in the Carolinas. She was an evangelist involved in healing ministries, and her book was called, "The Gift of Inner Healing." It was a God-inspired "how to" book about administering healing of inner traumas. I know it came under a lot of criticism by some of the leading Christians, but I found it interesting and very helpful as I have ministered to hurting people throughout the years. When a person has been wounded by someone or circumstances, they often face a mental block that doesn't let them emotionally get past the experience. As we grow from conception on, the clean slate we are given at birth gets written on with everything that happens around us and to us. It has been proven over and over that the fetus in the womb experiences what the mother feels, often making such an impression, that the child is wounded with the same problems mom faced until something changes that memory. They have even found that children in the womb who are read to and hear wonderful music will continue to desire that same kind of music and love of reading after they are born. There are many books written about this phenomena which should make a pregnant woman aware of the need to surround herself with positive attitudes, experiences and healthy living while carrying that child.

I bring this as part of the Thin Veil because I believe that the mind and its capabilities are part of that non-physical dimension that God can cross and change as we ask Him to. Praying for memories is a very interesting experience because God doesn't change the experience, but changes our memory of it. God is not a God limited to time, so time is not a barrier to Him. I will give you two examples of what I am talking about.

The first incident happened in California when I was visiting with one of my horse clients. After "chatting" with the horse, my client seemed hesitant to leave, so I asked her how I could help her. She told me the story of how her husband, the real love of her life, worked as an electrician. One day when he was on the line, he accidentally crossed the wrong line and was electrocuted. She was so devastated, she couldn't bring herself to even look at him burned and scarred, so she had a closed casket. This left her the feeling that he was still alive for that is the way she last saw him. A few years later, she married again, but said she just couldn't seem to let go of her dead husband and love the man she married. She admired him because he was a good man and very good to her, but her mind was blocked at the trauma she had experienced. We sat down together and as I laid hands on her, I asked the Holy Spirit to travel back in her mind to the day she said goodbye to him that morning. I then asked the Holy Spirit to hold her close as I directed her to walk into the morgue, pull the sheet back, look at him and kiss him goodbye. I then asked the Holy Spirit to change her memory so she could do this and to realize the Lord had His arms around her, holding her close to comfort her. As we went through the process, the flood of emotions broke and she sobbed her heart out. When the session was over, she was a changed woman. The emotional barrier was broken. She said she had felt the Lord there with her and knew that now she was free to love her present husband.

A second incident involved me. All my life, I believed that men had no capacity to love. I felt that their motives when relating to others were bound up in selfishness. When I married, I married a man from Germany who had grown up as a Hitler youth. He had been taught, and believed, that he was not obligated to love someone unless they did what he wanted. Interesting that I would marry a man that fit what I believed, although I wasn't aware of what I was doing. I wanted children more than anything, but in the third month of pregnancy, I would miscarry. This was devastating to me and I went from one doctor to another, one test after another, and no one could find a reason for it. After the 5th miscarriage, I went to prayer and fasting to find out what was wrong. I asked the Holy Spirit to go back through my memories and reveal to me what had caused my attitude about men, and why I could never carry a child past three months. To my amazement, He revealed it. When my mother was 3 months pregnant with me, as a fetus in the womb, I heard her say, "That sexist, selfish man made me pregnant. All he thinks about are his own desires. I don't want this baby and wish I could get rid of it." There it was, rejection at three months, and the idea that men didn't love but acted out of selfishness, caused me to reject the child that in my conscious mind I wanted, but subconsciously rejected. I asked the Holy Spirit to open my eyes of understanding so that I could see the love men were capable of. He did just that and I have never doubted it again. Unfortunately, I was too old by that time to bear children, and being single, I knew it would be hard to live the way I was living and raise a child alone. It took years before I could sit in church through a baby dedication, but God has gradually healed that pain, too. I know I have five children I will get to know and love when I get to heaven, which is comfort enough for me now. Since those early experiences, I have prayed over many people asking the Holy Spirit to go back in a person's life. I ask them to show me the incident that created the block in the inner healing (called the Word of Knowledge, which is one of the gifts of the Spirit); I "see" what it was, and then pray for God's release by changing the memory of what happened. The changes have been remarkable.

During this time, I attended a meeting where Dick Mills was ministering. He is an incredible man who has just about memorized the Bible. When people step forward, God gives him a verse to quote to them that fits their situation. I had never seen him before and he definitely didn't know me, so what happened next was astounding. He looked at me and quoted Isaiah 54:1-7, "Sing, O barren woman, you who never bore a child: burst into song, shout for joy, you who were never in labor; because more are the children of the desolate woman than of her who has a husband," says the Lord. "Enlarge the place of your tent, stretch your tent curtains wide, do not hold back; lengthen your cords, strengthen your stakes. For you will spread out to the right and to the left; your descendants will dispossess nations and settle in their desolate cities. Do not be afraid; you will not suffer shame. Do not fear disgrace; you will not be humiliated. You will forget the shame of your youth and remember no more the reproach of your widowhood. For your Maker is your husband the Lord Almighty is his name the Holy One of Israel is your Redeemer; he is called the God of all the earth. The Lord will call you back as if you were a wife deserted and distressed in spirit–a wife who married young, only to be rejected," says your God. "For a brief moment I abandoned you, but with deep compassion I will bring you back." He couldn't have been more accurate had he known me. God knew though, and since Dick knew God, he was able to deliver His message on target.

One day, I was reading the paper when I noticed an announcement for auditions where producers were looking for new singing talent. I applied and was chosen to do 13 recordings. After the contracts were signed, I learned that they wanted to make me like Marilyn Monroe or Jane Mansfield, a sex symbol who was a natural blond with blue eyes, had a perfect figure and was quite attractive. They were excited because I had the voice to go along with the looks, so they thought they had the full package to make a lot of money. Every day I showed up at the studio, they tried and tried to get me to pose for photos in revealing clothes or tried to get me to sleep with some executive producer that could back the production. I repeatedly refused because as a Christian,

I just couldn't disgrace my Lord and there was no way I was going to commit adultery no matter how badly I wanted that career. Besides, I looked at all those women who had lived that way and many of them were miserable and died horrible deaths. I felt I could do it without going that route, but my producers insisted. I remember one day a producer approached me and started to fondle me, telling me that I would do what he wanted or else. I walked over to his desk, grabbed the contract and tore it to pieces. Then I walked back to him and poured the pieces into his hand saying, "Here's your bed, you lie in it, I will not compromise my life with God for you or anyone." He was in such shock that he never said a word as I quietly turned and walked out. I can remember walking down Hollywood Boulevard with tears streaming down my face, asking God why? It felt that all my hopes and dreams were in shreds like the pieces of the contract.

I couldn't see how it could get worse or how I could ever succeed in television, but God had a better plan. As many of us desire, I wanted to perform in music and enjoy all the accolades that go with fame and financial security; but, God wanted me to totally rely on Him for

His perfect will that included great fame without compromising my morals as the world does. I had to learn that He and His angels could cross that Thin Veil, take care of me every step of the way, and bring His Plan to pass.

Word started spreading about my ability to talk with animals. Several local television shows such as AM Los Angeles and Regis Philbin had heard about my work and invited me to be on their show. That led to more and more interviews, but no matter how hard I tried, I couldn't get an agent to help me. I had tried to get on some of the national shows, but every one of them turned me down. One day, as I was sitting in my living room in Glendale where I was living at the time, two things happened to me that made a deep impression on my future. The first was when I was praying that God would send me a husband. I told Him the kind of professional, Godly man I wanted, but couldn't figure out why He didn't send him. All of a sudden I heard His voice ask me, "Do you think the kind of mate you want would want you the way you are?" I fully understood His question when I attended group meetings of single adults, who were also praying for someone special. I asked them the same question God asked me, "Do you think the mate you are asking for would want you as you are?" I've come to understand that it is more important to BE the right person than it is to ask for the right person. Boy, that woke me up and from then on, I really cleaned up my act. I haven't always remained perfect as the cares of life can sometimes be overwhelming, but I try. God knows what we need and He will bring the perfect mate in His own timing, when we are committed to His will and we are ready to become the helpmate that person needs too.

The second lesson I learned was that I didn't need an agent to succeed in the entertainment industry, or any aspect of what He was calling me to do, I only needed Him. One day, as I sat praying, I heard Him tell me, "Call the Mike Douglas show." Of course as is typical, I argued with God that I had already tried them, but they had turned me down. Quietly and gently, but emphatically, He repeated, "Call the Mike Douglas Show NOW." I did and to my amazement they had just hired a new booking person who had heard of me and immediately booked me on. I did five shows with them over the next couple of years and had the wonderful privilege of appearing with my heroes, Roy Rogers and Dale Evans. It was a delightful time.

Things took off from there as God opened doors with Him as my agent. He either brought them to me or would tell me when to contact the show I wanted to appear on. I sure spent a lot of time behind the wheel of my motor home or flying hundreds of thousands of miles to appear on TV shows all over the world, speaking at conferences, teaching and talking to groups of animals. I was going constantly and I loved every minute of it. I was learning to depend on God and Him alone as my source and my provider. I finally bought a home in North Hollywood so I could be near Church on the Way and the friends I was making there. Life was good. There were many instances that happened over the next few years concerning the Thin Veil, but they don't particularly follow a time line so I will relate them in the next chapter. Enjoy.

# CHAPTER 4

# MORE ENCOUNTERS

*I* was called to a home in Covina, California, one day to "chat" with some cats. When we were finished, the owner and I just sat and visited for awhile, something I loved to do in getting to know the person, not just the pets. She began to tell me that she had a poltergeist living in her house.

"What does it do, and how do you know it's there? Does it frighten you?"

"No, it doesn't scare me," she replied. "It's just kind of funny the tricks it pulls."

"What does it do?" I asked.

"Well, when I take a shower, I often have a cigarette with me. I light it, take a few puffs, and put it on the ashtray when I step into the shower. I never hear anything, but when I get out of the shower, the cigarette is lit on both ends. Other times, I'll put something down and when I come back to get it, it's gone. I have to go hunt for it and usually I find it, it was just moved. It never talks to me, or harms me, just pulls silly tricks on me."

We talked for awhile during which I told her it's really not a good thing for it to stay. God doesn't operate that way. He never frightens us, He doesn't move things around, and He only comes to help and rescue us, not play tricks. Since it's apparently not from God by its actions, I advised her to get rid of it. When she asked me how, I showed her by walking throughout the house saying, "If you are not from God, then in the Name of Jesus I command you to leave and not return."

A few days later she called me to tell me what happened after I left. The next morning, as she was driving to work, things were moving around in her car. She knew that the poltergeist was there with her, but when she got to town, it left her alone and never came back.

Another time I was on a search and rescue team in Northern New York State. A plane had crashed in the mountains; the dog on board showed up in town, but there was no sign of the plane or the dog's owner. The search party had taken over a vacant house that had belonged to a woman who was a recluse. She hardly ever left the house and rarely ever let anyone in. She had died, but no one seemed to want to buy the house, so it was made available to the search party. When I went up to bed that night, I was just starting to drift off to sleep when an angry woman's voice snarled at me and said, "Get out of my house." To which I responded, "It isn't yours anymore, you have no need of it, so in the name of Jesus, go where you are supposed to be and leave here." It became quiet so I claimed the Scripture in Psalm 4:8 that David wrote when he was being pursued by Saul, "I will lie down and sleep in peace, for you alone, O Lord make me dwell in safety." I had a very restful night and never heard her again. I have relied on that verse many, many times before and since then. God does take care of us.

One evening, I was invited to a friend's house to play some games. Little did I know until I got there, the game was a Ouija board. They thought it was funny that it would move when they touched it, not realizing it was an evil spirit moving it, but I knew that it was evil. One lady there admitted that she never went out of the house until she consulted it for guidance. They wouldn't believe me when I told them they shouldn't be letting an evil spirit guide their lives, so I took the board and told them I would prove what was behind it. As I held the piece that moved, I asked it, "In Jesus's Name, tell me your name," to which it replied, "Liar." Then I asked, "Where do you come from?" and it spelled out the word, "Hell."I noticed that as soon as I touched the piece, and during the process of asking those questions, it kept trying to go off the board like it was trying to get away from me. Finally, I said, "Why don't you want to work for me and why are you trying to get away from me?" "Because you love Jesus and the church," it spelled out. The people around me were in shock. One lady did admit that after she brought it into the house, she started hearing sounds like knocking, things were moved around by "themselves," and she did start to experience a lot of fear. My recommendation was to burn it because if she just threw it away, someone may find it and bring the same danger into their home that she had. We threw it in the fireplace to be sure it was destroyed and as it burned, everyone heard the most horrible blood curdling scream come from it. Everyone in the party was pretty freaked out and vowed to never get involved with things like that again. In some other instances I've been called in on, I have found that bringing any of the occultist and new age material into your home, can bring the same kinds of spirits with it. You may think it is just innocent curiosity, but the enemy of your soul, Satan, knows how to slip in unawares.

I started delving into some automatic writing one night. It is a method whereby you hold a pen or pencil loosely in your hand over a clean piece of paper. As you ask the "spirit" or whatever it is, questions, your pen will move and write things on the paper. It seemed innocent enough and kind of fun so I started by asking some simple questions like, "Who are you?" (She was female, but I don't remember her name.) "Are you alive here on earth?" "NO," she replied. I asked, "Where did you live when you were alive?" "Armenia." "When did you die?" I can't remember the exact date, but she wrote out a number in the 1700's. Then came the clincher. The last question I asked was, "What do you want?" To which she answered with a question, "May I enter you?" At that I flipped out and yelled, "NO!" I threw down the pen and never tried automatic writing again.

One time I was visiting with a lady in New York City who made her living by what she called, "healings." She said that a power came over her as she moved her hands up and down on the person and claimed that she felt the heat as the healing power went out of her to the individual. Since she practiced these sessions in her home, a one room apartment, she asked me to sit by the window, out of the way, while she treated a client. I sat quietly by the window, watching what was happening, when suddenly I "saw" a demon come in through the window. As it did, I commanded it in the Name of Jesus to leave. It looked at me and sneered, "You can't chase me away, she invited me in. I can't touch you, but you can't stop me when she asks me in." I "saw" it go over to the psychic healer, enter her, and use her to physically treat the client. This reminded me again of the Scripture that says, "Satan comes as an angel of light." He doesn't care what he does or who he helps as long as they belong to him and are deceived about Christ. I talked with her about her faith only to learn she thought Christ and the Christian principle were nonsense, just crutches people needed because they were weak and needed something to lean on. But she didn't just think it was nonsense, I felt a hatred there aimed at God that she would not allow to go away.

Thank God, spirits can't enter the Christian who is walking with the Lord unless they have permission. I'm glad He still protects us even when we are being foolish. I have learned that the way they are given permission is through Ouija boards, automatic writing, delving into "past lives," living in deliberate disobedience to God and living in sin. One aspect of the philosophy of reincarnation is delving into past lives. I believe that what you are reaching when you are attempting to do that is in reality an evil spirit impersonating someone in order to gain access to people living now. I believe that what makes this concept so appealing is the fact that when someone is told "who" they were in their past life, 99% of the time it is some famous person, and often times, the same famous person. How can that happen? Does the soul fragment before it comes back to enter several people? How many Cleopatra's can there be alive at the same time in several different living people? Satan is so deceptive; you must try the spirits as the Scripture says in 1 John 4:1-3. When you are in those "hypnotic regression states" where your *"past life person"* comes through, you leave yourself wide open for deception. Satan and his demons know exactly how to appeal to your ego. A spirit or a person can bypass your thinking mind while you are in those trances, and tell you anything. This happened to Edgar Cayce when he was in a trance. As he came out of it, the person asking questions claimed he carried on about reincarnation. When Cayce asked if he said all that, questioning what he had never said before, the facilitator said, "No, but you alluded to it." That was when Cayce got off on metaphysics instead of sticking to his readings that had, until then, coincided with the Bible.

Good angels, God's messengers, do not possess people, but move around us to help and rescue us. The Holy Spirit, not the angels, is the only One who rightfully can and does possess His children. Throughout the Bible you will see that evil spirits are the ones who can possess people with the end result of harming that individual physically or spiritually. Luke 9:37-42 is only one example. Remember, those spirits have been around since God created them so they know everything that has gone on with people for thousands of years. Of course they can tell us facts about anyone who lives in the present or the past. I think this is what happens with explorations into so called "past lives". These spirits can tell you anything that happened to anyone and make you believe you were that person in your past life. Read II Corinthians 11, especially verse 14 that says, "And no wonder, for Satan himself masquerades as an angel of light. It is not surprising, then, if his servants masquerade as servants of righteousness. Their end will be what their actions deserve." The whole goal of reincarnation philosophy is to keep coming back so you can pay for past mistakes and eventually get good enough to reach a state of Nirvana which is "a sea of nothingness." Who in the world wants to do that when we see in I Corinthians 2:9 and John 14 that we can't even imagine how wonderful it will be with Him someday. If we could have paid for our own sins, then Jesus would not have had to die on the cross. Remember how He prayed in the garden, Luke 22:42, "Father, if you are willing, take this cup from me; yet not my will, but yours be done." The cup was his suffering and death on the cross, temporary separation from the Father, and His venture into hell to pay for our sins. This is told in all four gospels near the end of each book. Remember, this is God in the flesh who could have called down legions of angels to rescue him, but by the fact that He submitted to go through what He did, cements the fact that He alone could pay the price for our sins (Ephesians 2:8, 9).

I was called to a home in Arcadia to find out why a cocker spaniel was acting so strangely. He would be lying on the couch napping when suddenly he would bolt upright, jump off the couch, and run to the center of the room barking vigorously. As suddenly as he started barking, he got quiet. He sat looking at something invisible, cocking his head from side-to-side, with his eyes glued to...? The dog would gradually watch whatever it was slowly ascend to the ceiling where it apparently disappeared. Then, like nothing ever happened, the dog returned to his lounging on the couch. It happened a couple of times in her bedroom when he would repeat the same action, and watch whatever it was gradually ascend and disappear. She never saw anything, but the dog obviously did. She called me to find out what the dog saw.

The dog told me that a man would suddenly appear in the room so he would run over to him and bark at this intruder who would put his finger over his mouth and tell the dog to be quiet. The man would then rise until he vanished through the ceiling, thus the reason his head and eyes would gradually look up. I could very clearly "see" the man through the dog's eyes so I described him. He was fairly young, probably in his late 30's, slender, and Caucasian with dark hair. "Oh," she exclaimed, "I know who it is! My husband is an importer of goods and he is gone a lot to foreign countries looking for new items. The man you are describing is my former neighbor, who was killed in an automobile accident a few months ago. He was a good friend who didn't want me to be alone while my husband was gone, so he bought the Cocker as a gift to keep me company." Was it really him coming to check on her or what? I don't know. Anyway, mystery solved.

I had two very strange situations that were very similar. The first one happened as I was traveling through southern Utah, in one of the semi-deserts just north of the Grand Canyon. I had my three German Shepherds and my Pomeranian with me, and since we had been driving for hours, I decided to pull over and let the dogs have a good run. I parked off the road, we all piled out and they took off across the desert. I had been walking for about ½-mile when I suddenly looked up and saw a vision? It was of a prehistoric terrain that I was walking straight into it. It was the weirdest feeling I ever had. I knew that if I continued, I would walk straight into that other dimension of a prehistoric time. It scared me that that door of entry might close and I might not find my way back out. I have learned to listen to things like this, so I called the dogs, turned, and quickly returned to the motor home. I got out of there pretty fast. You may think I am delusional, but it was very real to me. I saw it. I've driven back through that area later in life, but never experienced it again even though my husband Paul and I spent the night camping near that spot. I can't explain this happening, but it was very real.

I usually traveled with all four of my dogs in my camper, so I was never afraid. They had saved my life several times. Once I was heading east going through Nebraska on Highway 80, at about 1:00 in the morning. I spotted a car on the side of the road and as I passed, I noticed a woman bundled up with a couple of children in the back seat. I backed up to see if they needed help. It was a very cold night and no one was on the road. I just couldn't leave them stranded there without trying to help. A man approached the driver's side window and started to tell me he was out of gas. The three shepherds were lying quietly on the floor next to me, but it was so dark, they couldn't be seen from the outside. Suddenly, the passenger door started to open and all three of those dogs rose with three sets of pearly whites going for whoever was trying to sneak in that door. The door slammed and I never did see who was trying to get in. I realized this was a set up and without those dogs I probably wouldn't be here today.

A similar thing happened when I parked on the beach overnight in Monterey, California. I was asleep in the upper bunk over the cab when I had a sense something was wrong. There weren't any sounds other than the ocean, but I crept out of bed to peek around the curtains. The moon was full enough so I could see that I was surrounded by a gang of young people in their late teens and twenties, carrying crow bars, knives and guns. I could see one of them approach the back compartment with the intent of prying it open. All was quiet, until they touched the vehicle. Chaos broke loose as all my dogs went ballistic; two of them broke through the screen in the back window just over that compartment the guy was going to pry open and nearly got that thief in the head. It sounded like I had thirty of those big dogs in there, and who knows, maybe God amplified their voices because I had never heard their barks and growls sound so loud as they tore from one end of that 30-foot rig to the other. That gang ran yelling, "Get out of here, that rig is loaded with big dogs." After they left, everything quieted down and I went back to sleep with no further incidences. I'm telling you this so that you will be able to understand how safe I felt with those dogs, and you will better understand my second strange encounter.

It was late at night when I was traveling South on Hwy. 101 in southern Oregon. It had been a long day of lectures and talking to animals and I was so exhausted I was falling asleep at the wheel. It was very dark, no moon or lights of any kind as I traveled the coast where there was nothing but miles and miles of forests. I kept looking for a place to pull over and sleep for the night and finally spotted a clearing about 10 feet off the road. I pulled in, lowered the bed and took the dogs out for their last minute relief. A feeling of fear crept over me like I had never experienced before. Visions of being surrounded by evil people wielding axes, with the intent to smash my windows and bludgeon me and the dogs, just wouldn't leave my inner vision. I prayed and prayed as I really didn't want to drive on, I was *sooo* tired. It just didn't make any sense as nothing was visible even with my bright flashlight and the stillness was almost deafening. Slowly and carefully, I loaded the dogs back in the camper, got in the driver's seat and drove about another 8 miles before the feeling passed and I was able to find a nice, open spot along the beach. The night passed without incident. Was that God warning me that there were dangerous people lurking in those woods just waiting for me to go to sleep so we would be vulnerable and couldn't escape? I don't know, but the one thing I have learned in life is to ask God what I should do and obey Him. Don't question why, just obey. I had to leave the area. He and the angels could see what I couldn't, and I am sure that whether it was something bad that had happened in that spot years ago that I was feeling, or something that was going to happen to me. I don't know and I really don't care, I just know that God was protecting me and some danger was averted because I listened.

I know Satan wanted to kill those dogs to make me more vulnerable, especially when another miracle concerning those dogs happened on Highway 101, not too far from Folsom Prison, in Northern California. I had been working in San Francisco for several days and was heading home in the motor home with the dogs when they let me know they needed to go. I found a nice farm area just off the highway, where I could pull far enough up the dirt road to let the dogs out where they would be safe, or so I thought. No sooner had they gotten out, when a big rabbit appeared on a mound almost in front of them. Well, no dog can resist a rabbit popping up in front of them without giving a good chase. Off they went after that critter and no amount of calling or chasing could stop them. I know Satan had put that thing there because it didn't act like any other rabbit I had ever seen. Its natural instinct is to jump down the first hole it could reach, but instead it passed several entrances to its hole and headed straight for the freeway with all three of my shepherds after it. As they approached the freeway, the rabbit headed straight into traffic, again something unnatural for a rabbit to do, and when it reached the middle of the road, it vanished, not hit by a car, but it just vanished. My dogs never stopped as they kept going looking for that rabbit. Suddenly, they encountered a huge Semi speeding down the center lane. All I could do was cry out, "Jesus, Jesus, Jesus!" I stood there in horror as I SAW THOSE DOGS GO INTO THE SIDE OF THE SEMI'S WHEELS AND VANISH. I knew they had to be dead as there was no way they could have missed it, but to my utter joy and surprise, when the Semi passed, there they stood on the center divider, looking bewildered like how did I get here? They trotted back toward me, through heavy traffic, and *were never touched!* When I checked them over the only thing I found was a cut across Philea's chest where she had hit the barb wire fence that was lining the field before she entered the freeway. Even that was only a superficial cut. I am so grateful that God took care of them as I loved them and counted on them for company and protection. It seemed to happen the same way I had experienced being "transported" from the middle of the accident, to passing the pileup on freeway 10 in California. The dogs were just somehow transported to that center divider and slowly but safely walked back through the freeway traffic that was traveling over 60 miles an hour. No one attempted to slow down, or even acted like they saw any dogs on the road. <u>THAT IS GOD</u>!

In 1985, I moved to Oregon to get away from all the stress of trying to keep my animals, and find a place to live where I wouldn't be harassed by animal control. I eventually found the 20-acres of my dream just outside Oregon City. The minute I walked onto that property, I knew it was my home. After walking the property, anointing it and the house with oil and inviting the Holy Spirit to cleanse it, I settled in. Since I am a true, bona fide, died in the wool Night Owl, I spent nearly every night before bed, walking the property, enjoying the cool, fresh air that I could breathe, but not see (those of you who live in "smogsville" will understand). It was so quiet, such a wonderful time to talk to the Lord. On moonlight nights, I loved stopping to watch the deer grazing in my pasture and listening to the singing of the Coyotes. This went on for a couple of years before I met a minister's wife by the name of Fran. She claimed she had been abducted by aliens in a space ship, been tested on, and released. She told me about the many times she had experienced time lapses that she just couldn't account for, and there was something about seeing those beings outside her windows, looking in before those time lapses occurred. At first I thought she was just having delusions, until I met with a group of her friends who were claiming the same thing. I realized they were serious and really believed it had happened to them. I started hearing about it on the radio and other media, and thought I would check it out reading everything I could find on the subject. The more I looked into it, the more things started happening around my house. I began to experience time lapses where I would be watching a TV show and suddenly realize that I hadn't moved, nothing had happened, but it was two hours later. Things started disappearing like the big soup tureen, my camera, and several other important items. I was afraid of the dark and couldn't bring myself to go out at night for the walks I loved so much. Every night, I awoke at 2:30 am only to see orbs of light darting around my bedroom. I became so afraid that I didn't dare sleep in the dark, everything that I loved changed.

This went on for a couple of weeks until I found a book written by a Christian Evangelist who wrote about this kind of phenomena. He described the same things that were happening to me as being Satanic in nature because Satan's favorite game is to create fear. God doesn't try to scare us but comforts us. It dawned on me that he was right, so the next night when I awoke and saw the orbs of light, I said, "in the name of Jesus, I bind you and command you to leave my home, property and life. You have no place here as I belong to Christ, and so do the things you have been taking. As you leave, put my stuff back on your way out." Instantly the lights left, I went back to a peaceful sleep and from that night on, I never saw them again. I lost my fear of the dark and again enjoyed taking a walk before bed. All the things that had disappeared were back. Jan, who worked for me as a housekeeper, also knew things were missing and had hunted for them with me. She was as delighted as I was to see everything returned. It just made me realize what Jesus was talking about in John 10:10 when He told his disciples that, "the thief (referring to Satan) comes only to steal and kill and destroy, I have come that they may have life, and have it the fullest." I went back to some of those people who had claimed they had been abducted and told them of my experience, but they didn't want to believe me, not even the minister's wife when I gave her I John 4:1 that tells us, "Dear friends, do not believe every spirit, but test the spirits to see whether they are from God...." Maybe there is something titillating about thinking you met aliens, but they weren't interested in testing out what was going on. They wanted to believe it.

# CHAPTER 5

# THE HAND OF GOD

*N*ot more than a mile from my new home, I discovered a small Baptist church and started attending services. One Sunday, I noticed a very familiar name in the church bulletin —Hayford; he was the soloist for the service. Since Hayford isn't a common name, after the service I approached Paul Hayford to ask if he knew my Pastor Jack Hayford from Church on the Way in Van Nuys, California. "Yes," he replied. "Jack is my cousin." They didn't look anything alike as Jack was a tall, thin man with a baritone singing voice, and Paul was a short, little Irishman with a sweet Irish tenor voice. The only things they had in common were the disappearing acts their hair was doing on their foreheads, and the fact that they were both pastors:

Jack of a mega-church, and Paul of smaller, community churches. Over the next ten years, Paul, his wife Ida, and I became fast friends. We did everything together, went on cruises, traveled to Southern California, and just hung out. They raised Chihuahuas, but didn't know how to care for them in a crisis, but I did; I couldn't afford to hire anyone to do the repairs around the house, but Paul knew what to do, so we exchanged services. While I loved both of them dearly and counted them as my best friends, I did notice that Paul had the stubbornness and temper often attributed to the Irish. I remember one day as we were heading north in the motor home to catch an Alaskan cruise with Jack Hayford and company out of Vancouver, Canada, I was visiting with Ida up front while Paul was resting on a bed in the back. I remember remarking to her that I admired her ability to live with such a stubborn and opinionated man like Paul for over 50 years and that I could never be married to someone like him. I loved him as a friend, but could never tolerate anything more. Years later when we talked about it, he told me that he had heard those remarks and thought to himself, "Don't worry lady, it would never happen on my part either." God certainly has a sense of humor as He knew what was ahead for both of us. He must have been having a big laugh over that conversation.

During our friendship, I observed how carefully Paul tended to Ida no matter how ill she got. She was wheelchair-bound with Multiple Sclerosis for over 30 years, and often experienced days when she would not be able to wake up, soiled herself, and couldn't eat. He cleaned her up, fed her, and worked part-time to provide for the needs that Medicare didn't cover. He never complained, never said a bad word about her, although she complained about him. She made up lies about him saying he was sleeping with prostitutes, was a hypocrite and more, called all the church members telling them about his sins, but he never retaliated; instead, he made excuses for her saying it was the disease talking. Being so close to them, I did not see any of the things she was constantly accusing him of and was dumbfounded at the love and patience he showed her when she "railed" on him. I had never seen a man care for someone like that before. He was devastated when things got really bad, and he lost her after 52 years of marriage.

After losing Ida, Paul just couldn't handle pastoring anymore. He spent the next two years traveling all over the United States in his small RV, listening to the Bible on cassette tapes to soothe his soul and his wounded emotions. He shared the sights with his three Chihuahuas who kept him company. I missed the companionship I had enjoyed with both of them, and looked forward to Paul's phone calls that became more and more frequent.

In August 2002, I planned a cruise with some friends through the Panama Canal, but my roommate for the trip backed out and we had to find a replacement or pick up the extra cost ourselves. Paul had just returned to California to visit his daughter Mary Ellen. I figured we were friends enough to travel together as we had often done on cruises and in the motor home, so I called to see if he would like to do the trip. He was overjoyed to go as he had always wanted to see the Panama Canal. He said he would be in Oregon in a few days and he would come by to visit and cement our plans. I couldn't understand why I was so excited to see him. Everyone who knew us realized we had grown to love each other, but I didn't see it because I still thought of him as Ida's husband. As he drove down my long driveway, his little dogs recognized where they were and started screaming with excitement as I ran out to greet them. I gave him a big hug, the first time I had ever done that before, and I asked him to camp at my place for a few days to which he agreed.

We both loved to play cards, so one evening after we had eaten dinner, we sat down to a rousing game of racetrack rummy. Suddenly Paul stopped, laid his cards down, took a deep breath and told me a story. He said that he had been driving through the Carolinas when a doe with her fawn jumped in front of him and stood looking at him. Without thinking, he said, "Gee, I wish Bea were here to see this, she would love it." He recalled that he was shocked when he realized he'd said my name and not Ida's. As he thought about what he had done, it dawned on him that he had grown to love me and wanted to ask me to marry him, but he didn't know how to pop the question—he was terrified I would turn him down. He chose to take this moment to ask me to make the trip our honeymoon. Well, I was definitely in a state of shock, we had never even held hands before much less thought about marriage. I told him I would pray about it and give him an answer in a couple of days.

I recalled how Gideon in Judges 6:36-39 had put a fleece before God to get an answer, so I decided I would do the same. No matter how we feel, only God knows what is going to happen in the future. After my first marriage, I decided I would only say yes if God said yes. I didn't tell Paul what the fleece was, but asked him to talk to his children about our possible marriage and see how they reacted. I didn't want to come between him and his children because I knew how important they were to him. I decided that if they were for our marriage, then I would take that as a yes from God. When he called Mary Ellen, she broke into the hallelujah chorus in agreement: his other daughter Sherrolyn told him she was glad he was finally going to be happy. My nephew Richard, who I am very close to, also knew Paul and gave his hearty approval. It was a hasty preparation, but we were married on October 12, 2002.

Only God knew how to bring us together in a way that I would grow to trust Paul and not be afraid of marrying him. It took 10 years for that to happen, but I can sure see the hand of God working to bring it about when the time was right. I could also see the hand of God intervening in Paul's health. After we were married, I discovered that he had many cancerous tumors growing all over his chest, neck, and face. Thank God, I had the product that could remove them: it took about a month to get them all. As I took each one off, I could see the runner going several inches under the skin to form another tumor that protruded to the chest in another place. I am convinced, since he had been ignoring them, that it would not have been much longer before they spread to the internal organs and eventual death. I am so grateful God knows His perfect timing for us.

. We couldn't have been happier. We were perfectly matched, loved our dogs (and all animals), thoroughly enjoyed showing our dogs at dog shows, loved to travel, even enjoyed the same kinds of foods, and especially loved the Lord. What a joy it was to study the Bible together every day. He was an incredible Bible teacher. I learned more about the Lord and His Word through Paul than I did in my four years of Bible College training. Paul deeply respected and appreciated what God was doing through my work in natural healing and my communication with animals. He never tried to boss me around, we just knew what each other needed and tried to fulfill that need as best we could for the next nine years. He wasn't perfect by any means and neither was I, but he was perfect for me and I loved him with all my heart. For the first time in my life, I found someone who I believed truly loved me.

Besides his love for the Lord and me, the thing I admired most about this man was his mind. He had total recall. He couldn't forget anything he read or heard, no matter how hard he tried. He never had to take a test in school because he would read the text book at the beginning of the year and remember everything in it. He knew the material better than his teachers.

That incredible mind is what brought him to the Lord. His father was an avid atheist who would often stand on street corners in Salt Lake City, Utah, where he was born and raised, and spew out his hatred for God and his philosophies about atheism. Paul had been deeply indoctrinated in those ideas: he never attended church (except once as a child and was kicked out because he got into a fight with one of the other boys) and never read the Bible. He met Ida on the school bus and she challenged him to read it. He got a Bible and read it all the way through. Paul had an incredible memory and with it, began to find things that were predicted 400 years before they actually happened. He saw the predictions about Jesus in Isaiah and other Old Testament books written hundreds of years before they were fulfilled in the New Testament. In reading Job, one of the Bible's oldest books, written thousands of years ago, he saw how accurate the Bible was when he read in Chapter 38:4, "Where were you [Job] when I hung the world on nothing?" From "The Universe Confirms the Bible," Dr. Jason Lisle says, "Indeed, the earth does float in space. We now have pictures of the earth taken from space that show it floating in the cosmic void. The earth literally hangs on nothing, just as the Bible teaches." What better explanation could there be than God hung it there? Paul read in Psalms 8:8 about the fish following the "paths of the sea," which Paul connected to what he had learned in science about how animals follow migration paths through the sea, confirming what David knew over 2,000 years ago. Paul realized that the Bible was true and that he needed to accept Christ as His Savior, so he said he knelt in his father's woodshed and asked Christ into his heart. From that day on he sought to serve the Lord, and eventually had the great joy of leading his parents and brothers to the Lord as well. A few years after high school, as Ida's husband and a new father, Paul attended Multnomah School of the Bible and started the semester three weeks late. With the mind God had given him, he aced John G. Mitchell's course, something no one had ever been able to do before.

Through the years, he pastored several independent community churches, but didn't believe in being paid for his service, so he supported his family by working as a machinist. When he moved to San Diego, California, he was hired as a machinist at the Naval Base. One day, I asked him what he considered his greatest accomplishment in that trade besides being named man of the year out of 6,000 employees for 6 consecutive years. He recalled several parts he had designed and made such as heat shields that protected certain parts of planes. He did it in such a way that it made it possible to build those parts and repair the planes at the base instead of sending them to the aircraft's manufacturer, resulting in saving the government millions of dollars, but his greatest pride was in what he was able to do for the aircraft carriers and its pilots. They had a problem with the launch valve exploding as they were launching planes into the air. It didn't happen every time, but they never knew when it would occur. As it exploded, it launched the plane and the pilot into the sea and both were lost. They sent the blueprints to various engineers that worked for the government, but no one could figure out what was wrong. Finally, the captain of the base brought the blueprints to Paul, who was by then known to be the base "Problem Solver." He took the blueprints home and spent the evening studying them. As he went to bed, he committed it to the Lord in prayer and went to sleep. In the middle of the night he was awakened, as God often did to give him the answers. He got up, wrote down the answer and the following morning, went to work building the part correctly. They tested his prototype and it worked; from that day on, they never lost another plane or pilot during a launch. I wonder how many pilots knew who was responsible for saving their lives. When the Captain asked him how he did it, Paul said he replied with, "I prayed about it." Although he was proud of these accomplishments, his heart's desire was to give God the glory. He loved his work and the men who worked around him. Many of them became lifelong friends, especially the ones who found Christ as Savior when they attended his lunch hour Bible classes.

Now, you ask why I bring this all up and what does it have to do with the Thin Veil? Because of the years of abuse that I had suffered from my first husband, every relationship I had for the next 30 years ended because I would find something wrong with the man and run away. I know that subconsciously I was running out of fear of being hurt again, but God knew what to do even if I didn't. I am sure God planned for me to observe the years I spent watching Paul care for his wife like a child, never complaining but making excuses for her abuse of him, made me realize I could trust this man and overlook his faults. Had I met Paul in any other way, I would have run as I had in every other relationship. God knew that someday we would need each other in spite of what I had said to Ida that day during our trip in the motor home. God brought it about in a way that we could grow to love each other and I could see that he was a trustworthy man. I also related this background of Paul to you so that you could understand the strong bond that existed between us and the experiences we shared with the Thin Veil.

On one of our trips, we went to a conference in Ohio and then headed south on I-75 to visit some friends in Macon, Georgia, a small town just south of Atlanta. The traffic was very heavy with cars and big semi trucks flying by on both sides. Paul was driving the motor home and I was enjoying the scenery, when he motioned to me to look behind us. He said, "There is a big motor home following us for at least 13 miles now. No matter what lane I am in, he gets right behind me. I know he is following us." He hardly had the words out of his mouth when we suddenly noticed all the traffic around us was gone. The motor home began to shake so violently, Paul couldn't hold it from drifting into the fast lane, which had been full of big trucks but now was suddenly empty. This gave him enough time to slow down and steer it back across the center and right lanes to the shoulder of the road, and safely come to a stop. We were pretty shaken up. What surprised us most was that when we looked behind us, the motor home that had been following us had pulled over, too.

When we got out, Paul started looking at the tires because the motor home had acted like one of them blew, but they were fine. He crawled under the front to see if he could find out what caused the near tragedy, but found nothing wrong. As he stood up, the couple in the other motor home approached us. "I know exactly what happened," he said. "There is a bar under the front that stabilizes the wheels. It has a part in there that you can't see, that has gone bad. It happened to us on a curve in Alaska. If you drive slowly, under 50 miles an hour, you can make it to the next town and find the part. It is not expensive and is easy to replace." After he pointed it out to Paul, he said goodbye, and they both got back into their rig and waved goodbye as they pulled out. It wasn't until we got back on the road that we became aware of what had happened. We realized that as the couple started up the hill, they had just vanished from sight right in front of us. We believed God had sent a couple of angels. I had noticed how beautiful his clear blue eyes were and even when I talked about the two cats they had on their dashboard, she said very little, they had such a quiet demeanor. We remember feeling only gratitude and peace as we made our way down to Atlanta where we found the part. Sure enough, when Paul changed it, the old part was broken. Had we not encountered the "angels," we would never have found the problem and possibly been killed as we traveled west. We felt so blessed to think that God loved us enough to protect us by sending two angels in a big motor home to follow us for over 13 miles. I believe, too, they somehow kept the traffic away from us when our vehicle went out of control, for had they not cleared the way, we would have been hit by a big semi and probably killed.

After we got back to Oregon, an acquaintance of ours called to ask if we could help her. Her uncle had died and her aunt had been moved to a nursing home. She had been trying to clean out her house so they could sell it to pay for her aunt's care, but they were having trouble removing things. They had taken pictures of the interior of the house and when the pictures were developed, they found shadowy figures blocking the stairway. Whenever anyone touched the collection of belt buckles that had belonged to her uncle, they were so hot that the individual touching them would get burns and even blisters on their fingers. We didn't preach to people, but we did share the Lord and tried our best to walk the walk every day, no matter who was around us. She knew Paul and I were Christians, so she was wondering if there was anything we could do to rid the house of whatever was there. We agreed and a few days later, after praying and fasting, we met her at the house. As we went through the house exorcising what was there, we could feel it gradually leave, peace settled over the house, and everything became normal to the touch. She had no more problems cleaning the house and no problems selling it.

Paul and I were "joined at the hip" – we did everything together. Because we were so strong, even in our 70's, we tried to get on the television show, "Amazing Race." We knew we could keep up and we wanted the opportunity to travel to other countries. But they didn't realize that our advanced chronological years belied what we could really do, and they didn't call us.

When Paul first started having physical problems, I didn't think too much of it as he had always been very strong. We thought he'd get over this, too. The only physical problem he had had was with acid reflux since he was in his thirties, so when the doctor suggested he try Omeprazol, Prilosec, and Nexium (commonly known as protonix, which are designed to stop the body's production of hydrochloric acid in the stomach), we didn't think much of it because it was sold over the counter. It gave him relief so we were thrilled, not realizing this was his death sentence. After he had been on protonix for a couple of years, he began to experience the first side effect of the drug: malnutrition, low iron and calcium, in particular. I couldn't figure out why. I was feeding him good, nutritious food and lots of my supplements – we just didn't connect the problems with the pills. Unfortunately, without any hydrochloric acid in his stomach, he could no longer breakdown the calcium and proteins he consumed which resulted in malnutrition. Then one day he came staggering in with a heart attack. It shocked both of us because he had a strong, enlarged heart due to his athletic prowess in his younger days. (I later learned that a heart attack can become another side effect of protonix.) Then he suffered more and more side effects of the drug like ulcers in his esophagus and small intestine. We later learned that if the hospital we were connected with had sent him to a teaching hospital like OHSU (Oregon Health & Sciences University), or Legacy in Beaverton, the doctors could have performed a nuclear test. That test would have told them what was causing the over secretion of acid, and when corrected, would have cured the acid problem immediately. Our hospital didn't have privileges with OHSU or Legacy, so they never recommended it. As he suffered more and more side effects, all they did was pour more and more of the drug into his system as he got sicker and sicker. I was so scared! I slept in the motor home outside the hospital, not leaving his side for the next four months. Thirteen of their doctors and hospital personnel surrounded me and tried to talk me into removing his feeding tubes and let him starve to death as they knew he would never get well. How cruel. They were telling me to kill my best friend and the love of my life. Of course, they knew he would never get well. They had seen hundreds of others go through the same thing so instead of trying to find the cause of the reflux, they just poured that poison into their patients until they died. A tumor as small as a pea, or a hormone or nutritional imbalance can cause the acid reflux problem but no one seemed to care or know what the root of the problem was. I finally got Paul moved to Legacy Emanuel where they performed the nuclear test. They discovered a small growth on the end of the pancreas that had formed when a piece of the spleen (that had ruptured when he was in a car accident in his 30's) had migrated there and attached itself. That was when the acid reflux started, but by the time we learned what was going on, it was too late. During his bouts with bleeding, three doctors had performed surgery in that area, all of them saw the growth and yet not one of them removed it even though they knew it would cure the reflux problem. When I pointed out the warning on the box that said not to take that drug for longer than four months, they sloughed it off as meaning nothing. All they did was pour more and more protonix into him until they killed his liver and his kidneys (another side effect of those drugs), and finally him on Christmas day 2011. He had begged them to help him live, but to no avail. While I could almost hear the shouts of joy as the many he had led to Christ greeted him with "here he comes," as he stepped through the veil into his new life in Heaven, that Christmas day my life seemed to end. I didn't know how I could go on without him.

In September 2011, I lost my last sibling, my favorite brother; in October, I lost another dear friend; in November, I lost another of my closest friends of 40 years; and then, Paul in December. While all this was going on, our county changed the rules concerning kennels and came after me for those changes with trumped up charges, false accusations, and phony fines of over $9,000, and forced me to leave my dying husband to appear in court. At the same time, my business was failing and I couldn't pay the bills. I knew I'd be homeless again soon unless I got a miracle. I had known a lot of grief in my life, but nothing like this. On and on it went for nearly a year while county officials threatened to take all of my dogs, the only comfort and companionship I had left. It felt like Satan had unleashed all hell on me until one day I finally had a breakdown. I took a gun and decided I could no longer go on. I planned to kill each of my dogs and then myself. The scripture in Daniel 7:25 says, "He (Satan) will speak out against the Most High and wear down the saints of the Highest One...." It's true, because I was worn down to this breaking point. Just as I got the gun out, my friend Annmarie walked in and took the gun away from me. God had to have sent her or I would have ended it all. Apparently, God wasn't finished with me yet. This is when I experienced the next encounter with the Thin Veil.

I write health newsletters for my business which, in spite of my pain, I had to do during this time. As I was writing, I was in so much pain that I could barely see the screen for crying. All of a sudden, a little 2-inch by 2-inch picture that I have on my top shelf next to the computer flew off the shelf and hit me on the arm. I realized it didn't happen by accident; something or someone had to throw it across several feet in order for it to hit me. Had it just fallen, it would have simply dropped down on the desk below the shelf. This snapped me out of my deep grief and crying as I knew it was Paul. He was always telling me not to let my emotions get the best of me, but get on with it, whatever I had to do. This was his way of dealing with things that were out of his control, so I cleared my thoughts and was able to finish the newsletter.

I learned from the experience of Princessa, and now Paul, that God seems to allow them to cross the Veil in order to bring comfort, and to break the hold deepest times of grief have on us. The second incident occurred when I decided to go to a dog show to be with some of my friends with the hope that it would help distract some of my pain. I went to a show that Paul and I had gone to the year before, the last one we had enjoyed together. Things were a little better until everyone decided they had to go home, which left me in the motor home by myself for the rest of the day. I started to lose it, sobbing over missing him. I decided I would go through the small collection of books I keep in my RV cupboard with the hope of finding something to distract my emotions. I reached up and my hand fell on a book I had never seen before, nor could I remember meeting the author who apparently autographed it to me. It was titled, "Never Alone," a story about a young woman in Tampa, Florida, who had lost her husband to a car accident. She talked about her grief which echoed what I was experiencing. Her husband had crossed the Thin Veil to save her life several times, but what spoke to me the most, was the fact that he used her keys to do it. She always kept them in one place in the house so she could easily find them when she needed them, something I do, too. She said that one day she was heading out to the store, but the keys were missing. She searched everywhere only to later find them in the very place they should have been. Puzzled, she later learned that had she gone when she planned instead of being delayed by the missing keys, she would have been involved in an accident at the train crossing.

This kind of struck a chord with me as Paul had harped at me about the car keys, telling me repeatedly to take care of them since it would cost $250 to replace this particular type that is inserted in the ignition, but not with a key, it is electronic. During his illness, I kept the car at the hospital along with the motor home, so I could go home to take showers, catch up on mail, and wash clothes. One night, as I was home doing laundry, the keys disappeared. I searched everywhere for them, went through all the garbage, the laundry and every place I had been in the house that night. I drove the car home, so I knew they had to be there somewhere, but alas, no key. My friend Ann had found one that didn't work anymore, except to start the car but couldn't lock or unlock it, so I used that one to get back to the hospital. I took everything out of every closet in the motor home, shook out all the sheets and clothes, but no key. I keep my jewelry in a box next to my bed in the motor home. I had been in the box in the morning to get jewelry out to wear and there was nothing on top of it when I closed it. After reading the book, crying my eyes out,

I decided to at least change my clothes and put my jewelry back. When I opened the closet door, to my utter amazement, there were the missing keys sitting on top of the jewelry case. I then thought about the things that had been happening to me that morning and began to wonder if Paul was there trying to comfort me. He had a favorite hat that he had purchased in Hawaii on one of our trips. Every time I went in or out the door that day, I remember finding it lying on the top step. I picked it up every time and put it up out of the way, only to later find it on the step again. Now, I don't go seeking to talk to the dead, I am not sure it is right to do, but sometimes things happen we don't expect. In this case, I picked the hat up and stuffed it into a place it absolutely could not fall from. I said out loud, "Paul if that is you doing this to comfort me by letting me know you are still watching over me, could you put that hat down one more time, but Satan, if it is you, then in the Name of Jesus I command you to leave, you have no place here." Lo and behold, about ten minutes later, it was back on the step again. I never saw or heard it move, but there it was. This brought me a lot of comfort as I headed home later that night. This happened in February 2012.

On April 16, 2012, on what would have been Paul's 81$^{st}$ birthday, we celebrated a memorial service at the church we both loved, Christ the Vine Lutheran Church in Damascus, Oregon. I had a small table in front of the podium with his picture, his Bible, and his ashes, which were in a box I had covered with duct tape. He loved that stuff and seemed to repair almost everything with it. As the service progressed, all of a sudden everyone gasped because the table lit up with the brightest light I have ever seen, blinding out everything on the table. It was simply amazing. Everyone saw it and even when they took pictures, you couldn't see anything but that bright light. Soon after that, I was sitting in church really missing him, when I felt him slide into the pew next to me and put his arm around my shoulder. It was such a comfort.

Two other things happened that I am sure he had a part of. When I was sitting with him in the hospital, I placed his cell phone on the sink next to me. When I was preparing to leave that evening, I couldn't find it. I checked the floor, the dresser next to him, all my pockets, purse and everything I had with me, but to no avail. I thought that maybe in my stress, I wasn't thinking clearly and had just left it in the motor home, so when I went out for the night, I tore it apart looking for that phone. No phone. About six months after Paul's death my cell phone died. I really didn't have the money to buy another one and couldn't figure out how I was going to replace it. Now I have a recliner couch that Paul and I always sat on that seemed to swallow up everything we brought near it. I had reached down into it to retrieve the latest dropped knitting needle, pen or whatever, as I had done literally dozens of times and that phone was not there. The last time I had it was in the hospital room; I figured it had accidently fallen into the garbage receptacle that stood next to the sink and was forever gone. The day my phone died, that evening I reached into the couch to retrieve something, but instead of what I was looking for, my hand landed on Paul's cell phone. Why didn't I feel it the myriad of times I'd been in that exact same spot, it hadn't been there before. How did he do that, getting it from the hospital to the couch where I sit? I don't know, but I was grateful to get it back and two years later I am still using it.

During my last trip to the coast in the motor home, I misplaced my driving glasses. I again tore the motor home apart looking for them, but alas, no glasses. I thought that I had left them in the car and just forgot, so I moved everything in the car looking for them. No glasses. I was having some trouble driving with my bifocals and sure missed those driving glasses, so I prayed that somehow I could find them. On May 1, 2014, after they had been missing for about a year, I reached down to get my cup that was in the cup holder in my car, and there were the glasses sitting on top of the console right next to my seat. I was sure grateful to Paul, an angel, or whoever put them there, as it's now making my life a lot easier. Whoever it was, had to cross that Thin Veil.

The last time I experienced Paul was Thanksgiving day, 2013. I had been fighting deep depression for several weeks missing him, so I decided to get away and spend the day with some friends. It took an hour to drive back home and on a full Turkey and pie stomach, you can imagine how tired Ashley (my niece who came to live with me after Paul died) and I were. Needless to say, I was fighting sleep as I was driving, but Ashley succumbed to her heavy eyelids. I slipped in a CD that Paul and I had purchased on our last cruise, a musician we both loved. That was not a good thing to do, because all the depression I had been suffering came to a head and I totally lost it. I could barely see through the tears and was sobbing uncontrollably when suddenly the back window on the passenger side came down. Ashley woke up asking me why I had opened the back window, to which I replied, "I didn't. Besides it's too cold to open the windows." Since I have the controls in the door by my left hand, I reached over and closed the window. Within seconds, the window opened and again I closed it. When it happened the third time, I was wondering if it was Paul doing that to break my deep depression. As I closed it again I said, "Paul, if that is you, open the window one more time, and when I close it don't open it again, then I will know it is you. But, Satan, if this is you, then in the Name of Jesus, I command you to leave." It opened, I shut it, and this time it stayed shut. All of a sudden, I felt him blow on the back of my neck which made me start laughing. I said, "Ok this is getting kind of creepy, I'm alright now, so you can stop," He did, and that was the last time, to this date, that I have felt his presence or have I suffered from such depression again.

I don't know how he crossed the Thin Veil, how he can open a window, or bring items back that were missing in a building to be in my couch at just the right time, or how he can move the keys and put them on top of a box I had opened that morning, or how he can keep putting his hat back on the step, but I am grateful he did. My dog, and then my beloved husband, both came to me at the times I was suffering the most from their loss, and brought comfort only they could bring. Even though I know the Word of God and I know the Lord as my Savior, there has always been a nagging doubt that Jesus really wasn't God, and does life exist after we die. I know intellectually it is true, but it had always bothered me. After reading Josh McDowell's book, "More Than a Carpenter," any doubts I had that Jesus is God, are gone. The experiences I had with Paul and my dog Princessa, and then seeing the movie, "Heaven is for Real," have totally erased the doubts that there is life after this physical one. I know that someday, for sure, I will once again be with those I love so much.

# CHAPTER 6

# UNDERSTANDING THE MIND AND HOW THE HOLY SPIRIT USES IT

*A*lmost everyone has experienced some of the natural things the mind can do. How many times have you been thinking of someone and out of the blue, they call or show up at your door? The closer the bond you have with that other person, the more it will happen. I have that special bond with Dr. Marvin Cain, a genius in veterinary science, who taught me acupuncture. I knew he had the answer to what I was trying to figure out one day, but since he was traveling, I didn't know how to reach him. The phone rang and to my surprise it was him. He said, "What do you need Bea, I felt you thinking about me. Do you have a question?"

Of course he had the answer. This has happened often between us, a pretty special experience in my book. How many people have had the feeling that something was wrong at home, only to get there and find they had been burglarized, or someone had been hurt or sick. As we learn to respond to those feelings, they will happen more often and more clearly. These are normal human experiences, but there's a level that is greatly expanded when the Holy Spirit takes over your life. That's what has happened to me as I've learned to listen to the Spirit's voice, such as the time I delivered God's message to the lady in church who had just had a miscarriage. As I respond to His commands, it becomes easier and easier to hear Him and to understand what He wants.

Now, there is something <u>very, very important</u> you need to understand before I go on with the things I will share in this chapter. YOU MUST TEST THE SPIRITS AND NOT JUST RESPOND TO ANYTHING YOU "HEAR." BE SURE THAT WHAT YOU ARE HEARING IS COMING FROM GOD AND WITH HIS BLESSING, AS THERE ARE MANY SPIRITS OUT THERE THAT CAN DECEIVE YOU. I John 4:1-3 warns, "Dear friends, do not believe every spirit, but test the spirits to see whether they are from God, because many false prophets have gone out into the world. This is how you can recognize the Spirit of God; every spirit that acknowledges that Jesus Christ has come in the flesh is from God, but every spirit that does not acknowledge [the truth about] Jesus is not from God..." GOD WILL <u>NEVER</u> INSTRUCT YOU TO GO AGAINST WHAT HE SPEAKS OF IN HIS WORD. HE WILL NEVER TELL YOU TO DO ANYTHING THAT IS SINFUL OR BRINGS HARM TO ANYONE. But Satan will do everything he can to deceive you and make you think the mental message is from God as is explained in II Corinthians 11:13-15, "For such men are false apostles, deceitful workmen masquerading as apostles of Christ. And no wonder, for Satan himself masquerades as an angel of light. It is not surprising, then, if his servants masquerade as servants of righteousness...." As I explained in earlier chapters, Satan and one-third of the angels (now known as demons or evil spirits) under his command were cast out of heaven to wreak havoc on the earth (Isaiah 12:12-15); and explained again, along with his final defeat, in Revelations 12:7-13.

If you commit yourself to the Holy Spirit and ask him to control what you are receiving, He will protect your mind. Matthew 7:7-12 says, "Ask and it will be given to you; seek and you will find; knock and the door will be opened to you. For everyone who asks receives; he who seeks finds; and to him who knocks, the door will be opened. Which of you, if his son asks for bread, will give him a stone? Or if he asks for a fish, will give him a snake? If you, then, though you are evil, know how to give good gifts to your children, how much more will your Father in heaven give good gifts to those who ask him?" Some of what I experience is natural to all of us, but most comes from the guidance of the Holy Spirit—I seek only to do that which pleases Him.

Right after I turned my life over to the Holy Spirit, I told God that I would serve Him in this new dimension if He would make sure I was accurate. The prophets and Apostles weren't partly right, but were accurate in what they did and said; therefore, if I am to represent Him and allow Him to work through my mind and actions, I want to do the same. I believe He has honored that request. Now I will share with you how the mind works and how the Holy Spirit can use it. This is linked to the

Thin Veil because it is dealing on a spiritual level that you cannot see or touch, but it is there.

The mind knows no distance or space. As my husband Paul often explained to me, it works like a radio wave that is tuned into the frequency assigned to a particular station. If someone tells me that the animal or person I am trying to speak with is in New York when in reality they are in California, I won't find them because I need to "tune in" to their frequency, so to speak. I usually need the name of the person or animal in order to find them. I don't know why some come through clearer than others, but they do. I remember for a period of three months, whenever I tried to "find" animals in the Chicago area, it was like I was hitting a steel wall, I couldn't get through. Then one day it lifted and I was able to find the animals again. Thankfully that doesn't happen often.

I just need to know where they are so I know where to send my mind or focus my direction. This mental language, since it is transmitted in pictures and feelings, seldom in words, knows no cultural language barrier. It makes no difference who I am talking with, I can understand them. It reminds me of the universal language before the Tower of Babel. It is called in modern terms, "Remote viewing," but didn't Jesus do it as though it was not unusual? Read John 1:47-50, "When Jesus saw Nathanael approaching, he said of him, 'Here is a true Israelite, in whom there is nothing false.' 'How do you know me?' Nathanael asked. Jesus answered, 'I saw you while you were still under the fig tree before Philip called you.' Then Nathanael declared, 'Rabbi, you are the Son of God; you are the King of Israel.' Jesus said, 'You believe because I told you I saw you under the fig tree. You shall see greater things than that.'"

As news spread about my communication with animals, I received calls from people for help. I remember one day a mother in Apple Valley called me in a panic over her missing 15 year old daughter. She had stolen the family car and run away with her adult boyfriend. She wanted to know if I could tune in to her to see where she was and what her intentions were. I mentally called her by name and asked her to show me signs that the car was passing indicating the town they were entering. She showed me looking at a sign that said, "Entering El Paso". She was pretty scared and realized she had gotten into more than she had bargained for. She was thinking of calling home, but was scared her mother was going to yell at her for what she'd done. I told the mom to stay totally calm when her daughter called, and to tell her she loved her and that anyone can make a mistake: come on home and we can work out our problems. Be supportive, not condemning. I received a call the next day from the mom. She was boarding a plane, but wanted to tell me that her daughter had indeed called that morning from El Paso, Texas. The daughter said she was sorry and wanted to come home. The mom gave her love and support, as I had suggested, and she was on her way to El Paso to pick up her daughter and the car. That one ended well for both mother and daughter, because her daughter was still alive, well, and coming home.

I believe it is explained in John 14:12-21, "I tell you the truth, anyone who has faith in me will do what I have been doing. He will do even greater things than these, because I am going to the Father. You may ask anything IN MY NAME, and I will do it. If you love me, you will obey what I command. And I will ask the Father, and he will give you another COUNSELOR to be with you forever— the Spirit of Truth. The world cannot accept him because it neither sees Him nor knows Him. But you know Him, for He lives with you and will be in you.... He who loves me will be loved by my Father, and I too will love him and show myself to him." Further down in that passage Jesus says in verse 25, "All this I have spoken while still with you. But the Counselor, the Holy Spirit, whom the Father will send in my name, will teach you all things and will remind you of everything I have said to you."

The key to opening the door to receive His teaching in all things is to obey the Lord and do as He commands, never violating what He taught in the Bible, by the Name of Jesus and through the power of the Holy Spirit dwelling in us, we will do greater things than Jesus did. Why are they greater? Because He is doing them through sinful, common, ordinary, imperfect human beings like you and me. I liken it to someone cooking great meals in spite of the fact that the pot is broken. The story of David is comforting because although he committed murder and adultery, he repented and God called him "a man after God's own heart." Look at Paul in Acts. He did many horrible things like torturing and killing Christians, yet once he met the Lord, he was changed, and God chose him to do mighty things in Jesus's Name.

It amazes me how God can use me when I have done so many things that I know were wrong, or were just plain bad decisions because I didn't ask His guidance first. I am thankful for I John 1:9, "If we confess our sins, He is faithful and just to forgive us our sins and cleanse us from all unrighteousness." I am so grateful God knows our hearts. The Scripture says that we can do what Jesus did but only BY THE POWER OF THE HOLY SPIRIT WORKING THROUGH our imperfect, sinful nature, and ONLY BY THE NAME OF JESUS, not in our own strength.

I searched the Scriptures to see exactly what Jesus told us to do and found a very interesting passage in Mark 16:14-20, "Later Jesus appeared to the Eleven as they were eating.... He said to them, "Go into all the world and preach the good news to all <u>creation</u> *(interesting)*. <u>Whoever believes and is baptized will be saved, but whoever does not believe will be condemned. And these signs will accompany those who believe:</u> *(He is only talking about Christians who are obeying Him.)* <u>In my name they will drive out demons; they will speak in new tongues;</u> they will pick up snakes with their hands; and when they drink deadly poison, it will not hurt them at all. They <u>will place their hands on the sick people,</u> <u>and they will get well.</u>" After the Lord Jesus had spoken to them, He was taken up into heaven and He sat at the right hand of God. <u>Then the disciples went out and</u> <u>preached everywhere, and the Lord worked with them</u> <u>and confirmed His word by the signs that accompanied</u> <u>it.</u>" When I read this passage, I started searching the New Testament to see if this message was only for the eleven disciples; and, if we believe it was, then all the teachings of Christ were only for the disciples. I don't see where God tells us to go through and cut out portions of the word, but instead in II Timothy 3:16 it says, "<u>All</u> Scripture is inspired by God and is profitable for teaching, reproof, correction and training in righteousness." In Acts 2 at Pentecost, Peter is quoting Joel 2:28-29, telling us in v.14, "Fellow Jews and all of you who are in Jerusalem...." Verse 17 says, "He will pour out His Spirit on <u>all</u> mankind," not just the Jews or the disciples. Verse18, "Even on my servants, both men and women, I will pour out my Spirit in those days...." I think this pretty well covers everyone. He was telling the crowds that what was happening that day had been prophesied by Joel hundreds of years ago. I couldn't find any place where the gifts of the Spirit are to end. Look all through I Corinthians12:3-11, "Therefore, I make known to you that no one speaking by the Spirit of God says, 'Jesus is cursed,' and no one can say, 'Jesus is Lord,' except by the Holy Spirit. There are varieties of gifts, but the same Spirit. There are varieties of ministries, but the same Lord. There are varieties of effects, but the same God works all things in all men. Now to each one is given the manifestation of the Spirit for the common good. For to one is given the Word of wisdom through the Spirit; and to another, the Word of knowledge according to the same Spirit; to another, faith by the same Spirit; and to another, gifts of healing by the same Spirit; and to another, the effecting of miracles; and to another, prophecy; to another, the distinguishing of spirits; to another, various kinds of tongues; and to another, the interpretation of tongues.

But one and the same Spirit works all these things, distributing to each one individually just as He wills."

There is no mention of these gifts ending, but rather the Word tells us how they are to be administered and conducted. It is instructed in 1 Corinthians, Chapters 12, 13, and 14, especially 14:39, "…and do not forbid speaking in tongues. But everything should be done in an orderly manner." Maybe you haven't been given the gifts that God has called me to use, but He does have more gifts to give if you will just surrender yourself to God and allow Him to use you as HE SEES FIT AND WHERE HE NEEDS A WORKER to administer His service.

1.  We are to pray in the Spirit as the Lord directs. Other than that one time I talked about earlier in the book, I have not been told to pray in public. It is my prayer language and it's available to everyone for the building up of the body and each other. In Corinthians 14, Paul tells us that we can all speak in tongues, but the other gifts of the Spirit are given out to individuals as God chooses, like prophecy, teaching, healing, each fitting together to build up the body of Christ. As Jude 20 tells us, "…but you, dear friends, build yourselves up in the most holy faith and pray in the Holy Spirit." Tongues are not only the heavenly language used by the Holy Spirit to pray through us for someone or something, but they're also for the building up of our own faith.

2. As is mentioned in Mark 16:17, He cast out demons to free the innocent from their grip and told us to do the same. If you don't know Jesus as your Savior and the Holy Spirit isn't living in you, don't attempt to do exorcisms or command any spirit to leave, even if you do use Jesus's name. It usually won't work; in fact, it could even become detrimental. In Acts 19:13-16, "Some Jews who went around driving out evil spirits tried to invoke the name of the Lord Jesus over those who were demon-possessed. They would say, 'In the name of Jesus whom Paul preaches, I command you to come out.'" Seven sons of Sceva, a Jewish Chief Priest, were doing this. (Just because they are called pastors and priests, doesn't guarantee they know the Lord and carry His authority.) The evil spirit answered them, "Jesus I know and Paul I know about, but who are you?" Then the man who had the evil spirit jumped on them and over powered them all. He gave them such a beating that they ran out of the house naked and bleeding (Acts 19:13-16).

3. He laid hands on the sick and they got well. We are to anoint them with oil and <u>command</u> the diseases to

go. Where in the Bible does it command us to pray, "If it be your will Lord, heal this person?" When did Jesus or the Disciples ever do that? All I read is that Jesus and the disciples laid hands on the sick, and <u>commanded</u> the disease to go! What He does with the results of your prayer is up to Him, but to follow His example, command it to go. How He cures them is up to Him, we are just to obey and command healing in Jesus's Name. One of the things people often say when praying for someone in danger or ill health is, "Lord be with...!" Why do we ask the Lord to be with them since He has promised He will never leave or forsake any of His children as is stated in John 14:16, "And I will ask the Father, and He will give you another Counselor to be with you forever" — The Holy Spirit with Whom we are sealed and Who lives inside us. Again, in Hebrews 13:5-6, "...for He Himself has said, 'I will never desert you; nor will I ever forsake you. The Lord is my helper, I will not be afraid....'" All the ill person needs is to be reminded that the Holy Spirit is with them. They are not going through this alone. Before you pray over someone, ask the Lord to guide you so that you can pray on target.

When I pray for someone's healing, I often pray like this, "Holy Spirit, open their eyes of understanding so that they may "see" You and know You are here. Send your comforting angels to surround them and bring them comfort in a way that they can understand and know that it is from You as You heal them. IN JESUS'S NAME, HOLY SPIRIT, send your healing fire through their body and burn out every cell of disease that lurks there, and destroy it forever. Even as they awaken in the night, let them see You standing by them that they may know that You have not forsaken them nor have You left them at any time since You neither sleep or slumber. We will continue to thank You and praise You for Your care over them." When there is an emotional root to their disease, I pray first for the gift of knowledge that we may defeat the root that will in turn heal the disease. Of all illnesses, 85% have an emotional root which needs to be changed if they are to get well.**

4. He did remote vision so why is it unusual when we do it? When I first started out in my profession, I would say things like, "I feel the pain here or there," while

pointing to a part of my body. I went back to study biology so I could learn what was "there" and what I "saw" with my mind's eye. I wanted to know exactly which organ had a problem, and what the problem was. I remember one time a lady called me to see if I could determine why, every month, she became so violently ill. She couldn't stop throwing up and became so dehydrated she had to be hospitalized. What I "saw" was a piece of infected uterine tissue that had migrated from the uterus, where she was suffering from Endometriosis, and travelled up the fallopian tube. When it reached the opening between the ovaries and the tube, it migrated into the intestinal area. It attached itself to part of the intestinal wall, where it didn't belong. One of the phenomenon that happens when you transplant tissue from one part of the body to another is that the tissue you transplant does not take on the activity of the new surrounding tissue, but will continue to act as it did in its original place. Even though this was attached to the outside of the intestinal wall, every month it acted as it would in the uterus. Since it didn't belong where it was, it made her violently ill; only when it was removed, could she get well. This is basically the same thing that happened with my husband when part of his spleen attached itself to the end of his pancreas. It reacted like a spleen and caused the overproduction of acid. The doctors knew that when it was removed, he would be instantly healed. Unfortunately, they chose <u>not</u> to remove it.

5. He knew what other people were thinking. Mark 2:8, "Immediately Jesus knew in His spirit, that this was what they were thinking in their hearts...." Again, in Matthew 12:25, "Jesus knew their thoughts." This statement appears all through the Gospels. Yes, I can perceive the thoughts of others, but I never do it without a purpose. Many times, I have been hired to "speak to" or find out what a non-verbal person, or someone in a coma, is thinking with the purpose of helping that person or the hurting family surrounding them. Other than for the purpose of rendering comfort and aide, I never "ask" to know what a person is thinking; that is an invasion of privacy and I believe, is forbidden by God. I learned this the hard way one time when I was in a relationship with

a man I deeply loved. I was wondering what he was doing when I wasn't with him. Because of the deep emotional tie on my part, once I got into his head and "saw" what he was doing, I couldn't tune him out. It was like I opened a door in my mind that I couldn't shut. This eventually caused a rift between us and damaged the courtship so badly, it was destroyed. I believe God allowed it to teach me a very important lesson. His gifts are given to enable us to minister to hurting souls, not to snoop.

Work was scarce in Oregon, so once a month I traveled to Southern California in my motor home to work with animal groups and see individual clients out of a holistic veterinary clinic I was associated with in North Hollywood. One weekend, when I finished a horse group in San Diego, I noticed that I felt weak and was passing a copious amount of blood. I gradually worked my way back up to my friend's place in Northridge, California. She commented on how bloated, pale, and sweaty I had become. "What's wrong?" she asked. All I could think of was getting back to Oregon where I could rest and maybe see my own naturopathic physician, but God had other plans. I headed north, but before I even got out of town, God stopped me with a very loud and clear command, "Go to the vet clinic NOW!" I couldn't see any reason for me to go there, but by then I had learned to listen when God spoke that emphatically, so I turned around and went back to North Hollywood. As I walked into the clinic, one of the veterinarians looked at me in shock. I was feeling pretty sick by then and suddenly started throwing up large amounts of blood. At that point, I felt a bump and realized I was looking down on my body watching John Ottaviano, a human and animal acupuncturist, work on me. I heard him say, "Her heart has stopped, I'll stimulate her heart points while you call 9-1-1." When he inserted the needles, I suddenly didn't see anything anymore. The next time I woke up, I was in the ambulance with the paramedics working on me. God knew what He was doing, because had He not warned me and had I not listened, I would have been on the I-5 somewhere in the San Joaquin Valley, and would have died. He was obviously not finished with me yet.

I was very close to Bill and Helen Thompson, who lived in Northridge, California, a town in the San Fernando Valley where I lived for many years. We worked together rescuing animals and rehabilitating them and our bond was very special. The one thing we differed on was how we related to God. I am a strong Christian with God as the focus of my life, but they wanted nothing to do with God. They said they were basically atheists. Helen's mother, Lottie, who was from Germany, often visited them when I was there, so I got to know her well. I was at home in Portland when Helen called me asking if I was coming down their way anytime soon. She said that her mother was in the hospital dying of liver cancer, but she had a problem and wanted to know if I could come right away and help her. She said her mother was refusing to let go and leave her body because every time she did, she acted terrified. Since Lottie was non-verbal, no one could figure out why. Helen wanted me to talk to her mentally and find out what was going on.

As I drove south, I spent the next 24 hours fasting and praying. I knew that Lottie was dealing with a spiritual problem, but with Helen refusing to acknowledge there was a God, I knew she would not allow me to speak to her mom about her spiritual condition. God would have to get Helen out of the hospital room long enough to allow me time to speak to Lottie about the Lord. I parked the motor home in visitor parking, and as I went upstairs, Helen went down, looking for me in the parking lot. All the nurses left as I entered the room, leaving Lottie and I alone. I asked her what her fear was. This is what she told me mentally. As she was leaving her body, she felt like she was being pulled into a gaping hole that was very lit up, with horrible voices coming out of it. She was terrified.

In all the years I've watched movies, the best example of the truth about heaven and hell was exemplified in the movie "Ghost," when Patrick Swayze was standing on the street and souls were either going up in peace or were dying and being sucked into hell, screaming in terror. Whoever wrote that film must have been a Christian, because what they described is real from those I have witnessed dying.

Standing to Lottie's right and just above her, was a man watching her being drawn toward the hole with tears running down his face and two angels standing, one on each side of him. She kept fighting going into the hole. I told her that was hell and because of her rejection of Christ as her Savior, she was going there. I shared the love of Jesus and His forgiveness of her sins, if she would just accept what He had done for her on the Cross, confess her sins and ask Him into her heart, she would be saved from going into hell and could join that man and Jesus in heaven. Tears were in her eyes as she communicated, "It is too late." I told her it wasn't too late because she was still alive, but it would be too late if she continued to reject Christ until she died. In her heart, she prayed with me for God to forgive her and come into her heart. As she prayed, such a peace came over her face and all the fear left. Just as we finished praying, Helen came back into the room. We visited for awhile and as I left, I handed Helen a Bible and said, "I have marked some passages like Psalm 23 that I want you to read to her," to which Helen snickered and said, "She doesn't want that, she doesn't believe in the Bible." I replied, as I left the room, "She does now."

A few days later, I stopped over for a visit with Helen. She told me that after I left, her mother was so at peace, no one could believe the change, and that she had slipped away easily and quietly. I then told her what had happened and that her mother had accepted Christ and found His forgiveness and peace. She didn't say much but went to get a family album. As she opened it, she asked me if any of the people in the album looked like the man with the tears in his eyes. I flipped the pages and I pointed out the man I saw. It turned out to be Lottie's father, a man Helen remembered as being very religious.

The story doesn't end there. A few years later, I was visiting with Helen when she turned to me and said, "I have often thought about what you saw and did with my mother. I believe that was real and I wanted to know how I can have Jesus as My Savior, too?" What a joy it was to lead my best friend to Christ, knowing that when she died a year later, she was having a reunion with her mom and grandfather, and I'll see her again when I get there. All of this happened because I was obedient to the Holy Spirit when He asked me to use the gift of communication to reach non-verbal people for Him. Had I not obeyed, Helen and her mom would now be in hell. Believe me, Heaven is for real, but so is Hell, and everyone is not at peace when they leave this life. You may not believe in God, but you will when you leave your body.

I found that there is a difference between what I experienced with Lottie and what happened with my dogs. I had three German Shepherds—the mother, Princess; her daughter, Philea; and her son, Loverboy. I don't think I have ever found three dogs more bonded. Due to an inherited degenerative disease called Myleopathy, which is similar to Multiple Sclerosis in people, the mother and daughter were euthanized at the same time. Loverboy was also suffering from the same disease, but it hadn't progressed as far as it had in his mother and sister, so I only put the two of them to sleep and kept him. He was very upset with me as he had wanted to go with them. He moped and became so depressed that he even quit walking, so I decided to let him go because he was asking me to release him. These were three of my favorite dogs, but because I loved them so, I couldn't make him suffer anymore. While he was leaving his body, I could "see" the joyous reunion as they trotted off with Loverboy between the two of them. He didn't even look back to say goodbye, all he wanted was to be with them. I could see such a beautiful place in the distance so I asked God if I could "see" a little further, I wanted to follow them for awhile. This is exactly what He told me. "If you go any further, you won't be able to come back." I knew He had much more for me to do, so I had to be content in "seeing" them so healthy and happy. I have come to understand that what I "saw" was different from the out of body experiences people have where they literally leave an injured or ill body and go somewhere like the little boy in the movie, "Heaven Is For Real." I was not ill, my body was fine, so I was only allowed to "see" a short distance.

Unlike Loverboy who wanted to go with his family, there are those who experience passing over differently. Take for instance a case I was working on in Washington. A man called asking for help because his dog was missing and he couldn't find her. I put myself into the lost animal's body and listened for sounds and sights that were around her so I could give the owner some indication of where she may be. He started from his home and gradually fanned out across the countryside.

When I could hear him calling (from the dog's ears), I guided him on his cell phone by telling him when his voice got louder indicating he was getting closer to her. Finally, he ended up by the bridge near the road, but couldn't see the dog. We were puzzled because she kept telling me that he was standing right over her, but he couldn't see her. Nothing was there! I was really baffled over it until a few days later when he called me to tell me that someone had hit and killed his dog in the very spot he had been standing in, directly over her. The person who hit her with their car, picked up her body and dumped it where someone found it and called him. As I thought about it, I realized a phenomenon I had observed before. It seems that when a person or animal is killed in an accident, it sometimes takes time for them to realize they are dead, thus the dog thought she was still in the spot where her spirit left her body.

I was working on a missing man in the Cascades, about an hour from home. I was able to tell the searchers what had happened and even lead them in the direction he went through the woods. His camp was found several miles back in the woods to a place where people commonly camped by a small, hidden lake. This man had set up camp and disappeared. The day the searchers took me down there on an ATV, it was already getting late in the day, and we had to quit in order to get out safely before dark. They planned to go back out the next morning at daybreak, but because I lived an hour away and had no one at the house to care for the animals, I had to go home. I arrived back at base camp the next day just after the search party had left the staging area, and no one would take me back out on the mountain so I could continue to track him. I was getting pretty distraught because he kept calling me mentally to help him. He told me he had fallen over a small embankment and had broken his leg so he couldn't get himself out. They didn't find him, but for the next three days, his calling kept me awake as I felt more and more of his desperation. Then it faded and I knew he died. That was very hard for me to handle, feeling someone's desperation, and then feeling him die. You see, when I opened myself up to him to obtain information to help the searchers find him, his pain and desperation prevented me from tuning him out until he died. That kind of situation is very hard on me because I feel what he is going through. I have worked on many other cases of lost people, some I have been able to help and others not, but since I feel what they are going through, it is very hard on me. I quit doing it most of the time because law enforcement or search teams often just won't listen, and I can't go hiking up mountains to find them on my own by myself, but I do help when I can. When I am able to make a difference, it is a real blessing to help; but when I can't, as was the case with this missing man (to my knowledge they never found his body), it is almost like a curse.

6. Jesus had power over the wind and even quieted the seas. Since I can do what He did, I took God literally at His Word believing that in some circumstances I could do that, too. One day it was announced on the news that a very violent wind and rain storm was coming. Well, if you have ever lived in the Portland, Oregon area, you would know that the wind doesn't have to be violent to shut the electricity off and the roads become blocked with fallen trees and debris. All it takes is just a good breeze. I was very short on funds and couldn't afford the repairs that would be needed as a result of a violent wind, so I stood on my

front deck and rebuked the storm from my 20 acres, asking God to take the storm around me and leave us safe. I didn't think anything more about it, went on about my business, and figured the storm didn't happen since it was so quiet. Boy was I surprised when I later went outside and found incredible devastation all around my property, but on my property, barely a leaf down.

This same thing happened on several other occasions, like the time I was driving my motor home through Utah when a tornado came across my path. I rebuked the storm and prayed that it would go around the motor home and it did. We barely felt the wind. When driving in bad weather or high winds, a motor home has a pretty wide surface for the wind to push and because it is lighter than the big Semi trucks, it is more easily blown over. We have that privilege and safety in Christ, to call on His protection and rebuke nature. I wish I could remember to pray that way and speak to the storm at other times when terrible things have happened, but it is easy to forget.

7. He ministered with compassion to the sick and sorrowing. I believe that we are all called to do that. It doesn't always involve money, but it does involve our time and love. I have had several instances when a person was either in a coma or paralyzed, and couldn't speak or express themselves. Their minds are still alive and active and they are able to tell me what they need, want, or are frustrated about. It is a great time to minister to the families and help relieve suffering. You can express God's love in many other ways such as just picking up the phone to call a shut-in or a lonely person to brighten their day; taking a small bouquet of flowers to someone who doesn't have a family to attend to them; or, buying a meal for a homeless, hungry person you pass on the street. I remember one night, sitting in my car at a Wendy's, eating a burger. A man stopped to ask for some food, but I sent him away knowing I had the means to buy him what he needed. I wonder if that stranger was sent by God to teach me compassion as is expressed in Hebrews 13:1-2, "Keep on loving each other as brothers. Do not forget to entertain strangers, for by so doing some people

have entertained angels without knowing it." I will NEVER forget the look of sadness in his eyes as he starred at me for a few minutes and with hunched over shoulders, walked away. <u>Those eyes haunt me to this day</u>. Whenever I see a person begging for help, I now offer to buy them a meal or get them some food; I don't give money that could be used for other purposes like liquor or drugs. I believe God sends certain people our way because He knows we have the capacity to relieve their sufferings and minister the Gospel to them. We are His representatives to the hurting. When we fail to help that one, we miss the Blessings God intended to give us. There is joy in giving.

I believe we are to exercise the gifts of the Holy Spirit as He leads us. Not everyone is to be a teacher, not everyone is to exercise the Word of Knowledge, but I believe He does give us all the gift of Discernment—that is, to know right from wrong, and to know <u>what</u> spirit is leading us. When we are "getting out of bounds of His Will," the Holy Spirit will give us a check in our Spirit and we will know something is wrong, or we are to stop what we are doing. This happened often in the formulation of my products. One time I was working on a Heart and Blood Vessel formula when I had a strong check in my spirit. I left the formula in the blender until I had a chance to pray about it overnight. The answer came to me the next morning, and I knew I had to double all the ingredients except one to get it in balance. I obeyed, blended it, and it worked perfectly. I am grateful God did that because that one formula saved my life when I went into Atrial Fibrillation. Now all I have to do is take one capsule a day of those safe herbs, and it no longer bothers me. Before I made any of my formulas, I prayed and fasted for God's knowledge. When they were right, the Holy Spirit gave me the peace I needed to finish them. I had no idea these products were going to do the healing they have, but I obeyed His leading and He took care of the rest. They saved my life and the lives of hundreds of people and animals who have used them.

Sometimes when I see someone, my spirit leaps within me and I know it is the Holy Spirit telling me something is wrong with them. I believe those times are a call for me to pray for that person, as God doesn't tell me what is wrong, but that I am to pray in the Spirit for

He knows what to pray. This has happened several times with televangelists that I have seen, only to later learn that they had fallen into sin and lost or damaged their ministry. God is not a gossiper. He isn't telling us secrets to titillate our curiosity, but He is doing it as a call to prayer. It also happened once when I looked at a music minister of a large church. I never saw anything happen, but I knew something was wrong and God was calling me to pray for that person. These incidents are damaging to the Gospel and I am sure it grieves the Father greatly.

These revelations happen a lot concerning children, mostly during dedications, baptisms and confirmations. As I look at each child, I can see what their problems will be and how Satan seeks to destroy them. Again, it is a call to pray earnestly for them that God will block the darts of the evil one from what he intends to do to destroy that child's future.

I believe this is called, "Praying without ceasing" (I Thessalonians 5:17). As God shows us something, we are to stop a moment and utter a prayer for that loved one, or that circumstance. We are to do that many times throughout the day, as God quickens our hearts. It may be the person we see crossing the street, a homeless person walking by, or a person in a car that passes dangerously fast that needs intercession. We are not to only designate a set period of time each day to pray, but to pray for whomever or whatever we see around us as the Spirit prompts us. In the same way, we have access to the Father at any moment of any day to intercede for someone, we also have access to Him 24/7 just to talk to Him—He is always with you. When I misplace something and can't remember where I put it, I just tell the Holy Spirit (because He is with me) to remind me where I put it. He doesn't have the forgetfulness I do and since He was there when I put it down, He knows where it is. Usually within minutes, He will quicken my mind where to look and sure enough it is there. If I were to look without asking Him, it would take hours and I may never find it. He is a close friend who is all-knowing, so why not talk to Him as you would a friend you are hanging out with! Since God made us for fellowship with Him as it says in Genesis 1, and He is living inside us, then I believe He is to be an everyday part of my life, even more so than a spouse or child. I believe He is interested in every aspect of our lives. He knows our hurts, our fears, disappointments, dreams, and difficulties, so give Him access to them by talking to Him. Tell Him how you feel. He will understand. Ask Him for help, He will. You don't sit the Holy Spirit down in the pew when you leave church on Sunday and tell Him you'll see Him next week. No. Take Him home with you, make Him an integral part of your life. Don't just ask Him to intervene in circumstances, but do as Jesus did, defeat Satan by the Word of God. He has given us authority in the Name of Jesus to control our circumstances as it says in Matthew 18:18, "I tell you the truth, whatever you bind on earth will be bound in heaven, and whatever you loose on earth will be loosed in heaven." Again, in Matthew 16:18,19, He may have been talking to Peter, however the rock He was referring to was not Peter himself, but Peter's confession that Jesus is the Christ, the Son of God "upon this rock I will build my church and the gates of Hades will not overcome it. I will give you the keys of the kingdom of heaven: whatever you bind on earth will be bound in heaven, and whatever you loose on earth will be loosed in heaven."

I have known this verse and stood on it hundreds of times, but sometimes the burdens of the cares of life will gradually wear you down, and you forget and stop fighting the spiritual battle. Sometimes you get too weary, and you get lax about standing up and fighting. We really don't have that luxury because Satan will take advantage and really come after us. We have a determined adversary, who is out to destroy us. As Ephesians 6:12 tells us, "For our struggle is not against flesh and blood, but against the rulers, against the authorities, against the powers of this dark world and against the spiritual forces of evil in the heavenly realms." Are you having financial problems? <u>Bind</u> Satan who comes to steal in the Name of Jesus, and <u>loose</u> the Holy Spirit to go out and bring in what you need. He promised in Philippians 4:19, "And my God will supply all your needs according to His riches in Glory in Christ Jesus." Remember, Jesus taught us to ask Him for help when He taught us how to pray in the Lord's Prayer. God has plenty of resources, He isn't poor. I have done this every time the finances have gotten bad and He always comes through. Again, in I Peter 5:6 and 7, "Therefore humble yourselves under the mighty hand of God, that He may exalt you at the proper time, casting all your anxiety on Him, because He cares for you." This is hard to do when your home or business is in jeopardy, and we forget to have the faith that He will bring us through. Having problems in your relationships? In Jesus's Name, bind the enemy who is trying to divide you and ask the Holy Spirit to bring you peace. Recently, I had been having a terrible time going to sleep and started taking things to help me. My dreams were full of horrible nightmares until someone reminded me of the authority we have in Christ to bind the enemy. I started doing that and asking the Holy Spirit to come and bring me good sleep. Every night when I do that before bed, my problems are all solved; I go to sleep quickly, have pleasant dreams and wake up refreshed. Take your stand in whatever circumstance you are in and remember, the Holy Spirit <u>lives</u> in us, but He chooses to work through us.

Since Jesus sent the Holy Spirit to comfort us, to teach us, and to lead us into all truth, why is it so surprising that when I told God I would do whatever He wanted me to do no matter what it involved, that He would teach me the secrets of God? You and I are no different from the Disciples or anyone else who gave themselves wholly to serve the Lord without reservation. If you are willing to step out of the norm in life, He will use you in ways that will surprise you. A long time ago, when I was so ill, bedridden 23 out of 24 hours a day, loaded with viruses, parasites and tumors, I thought I was going to die. As I lay before the Lord, I cried out for help. He spoke clearly to me, "I know what is wrong and what man did to create this problem, (for millions of people, not just me). If you will let me teach you, I will show you how to fix it." That is when He guided me through prayer and fasting to create the Herbal formulas that led to my recovery from the Simian 40 virus known as Fibromyalgia, Hepatitis C, Lupus, HIV and many other diseases. The story is explained clearly in my book, "Seasons, My Journey through the Three Dimensions of Natural Healing." It blows my mind when people act surprised that I can clear up diseases that even the doctors in reality know nothing about. Don't they realize the God of the Universe Who promised to teach us and lead us into All Truth would know how to fix them? It isn't my knowledge because I would not know these truths unless they were taught to me by my Lord who quickened my mind to understand them. Man is so tied into Pharmacopeia, called witchcraft in the Bible, that he can't see the miracles and wisdom of God?

Whether man chooses to believe me or not, over 90% of those who come to me are getting well from most major diseases. It is not important to me what anyone believes or not, I know Who taught them to me and as long as I do what He wants, that is all that matters to me. It is their loss, not mine, for I am well; I work full time, I show dogs on weekends, I'm involved in my church as much as time will allow, and I travel whenever I can, dogs in tow. I wish I could say I always follow the instructions I have shared with you in this chapter, but unfortunately I forget too easily. I am a work in progress and probably will be until I step out of my body through the Thin Veil.

# CHAPTER 7

# CHRISTMAS 2013

As the holidays approached, instead of the joy of celebrating the season, I was looking forward to it with dread because it would be the second anniversary of Paul leaving this earth. I had been in deep depression for about two weeks until the incident in the car on my way home Thanksgiving evening when Paul came to comfort me. I decided I had better snap out of it and decide how I could make the Christmas season, especially Christmas day, a fitting memorial rather than a day of grieving. Since I was going to be by myself this year, I decided that instead of giving things, I would give of myself in caring for others. The food bank at the church had been given an over abundance of food, so I asked if they would allow me to go out into some of the local trailer parks where I knew people who had very little. They agreed and I spent several days delivering food, and sharing the love of Christ with a lot of hurting people who were very grateful to have enough to eat. Then I invited a friend who was having some problems and had no special person to spend the holidays with, to come join me in distributing food and sharing Christmas dinner. He is a long-haul trucker based in the Mid-West. He asked his company to give him a load to the west coast, and lo and behold, they had one that needed to be delivered the day after Christmas. We had a wonderful time, enjoyed good food, and spent time with his sweet traveling companion, Miss Kitty Cleo. When he left, I was exhausted from all the activities, but it turned out to be one of the best Christmases I could remember.

Over the years, I have heard the Christmas Story read over and over and interpreted in so many ways. I can practically quote it word for word, so I asked God to give me a "fresh look" at what Christmas means to us, His children. I just wanted to get a different take on how God sees Christmas. Here is what He revealed to me that has made the Birth of Christ even more personal.

As my pastor was reading on Christmas Eve, I suddenly saw a whole new dimension to the story. I realized Christmas is more than the Birth of Jesus, it is also about <u>Obedience and Timing</u>. I would like to bring the story to you in modern day.

What if God did today what He did then, would it have made an impact on our world? I don't think so because in our modern society, an unwed teenage mother would just be another pregnancy as far as the world is concerned, no big deal. Even as she was showing, she may have gone on to graduate from High School or she may have even aborted Him because the timing was bad. We pray for God to send us people to perform great deeds like finding a cure for Cancer, Multiple Sclerosis (MS) or Amyotrophic Lateral Sclerosis (ALS), yet when He does, the woman carrying that answer to world problems didn't want the child and aborted it. Had Jesus been born today, they would have whisked the mother away on a gurney to have the baby in a sterile, warm, clean environment delivered by a Pediatrician and nurses to take care of her and the newborn. No, God's timing is perfect. He knew best when He had to arrive.

Now, take Mary for instance. When the angel came to her and announced that she would have a baby, in those days, as an engaged woman found with child, she would have been sent away and probably stoned to death as an adulterous woman. How many of us would have said yes to that kind of danger when half the time we are too busy to walk across the street and minister to a hurting neighbor! We read the story like it is ho-hum, yet Mary said okay to the angel. Do we have any idea what it meant to say yes back in those days? What would you have done? How would you have reacted? If that happened to me, I think I would have stood there and looked around asking, "uh, are you talking to "moi" and you want me to do what? Stick my ever loving neck out for what? A Virgin Birth? Ohhhhh kayyyyyyyyy. What does that mean and what am I going to get into?" I wonder if Mary was scared. She didn't know how Joseph would react and what she was getting into. I just don't see how any 16 year old girl, especially under the cultural conditions of that day or today, no matter how pious, would just jump up and say "sure God."

Here is the point. <u>WHAT IF SHE HAD NOT OBEYED?</u> <u>We wouldn't have even had a Christmas to</u>

<u>read about.</u> I'm sure God could have found another way to bring His Son into the world, but He didn't have to because she obeyed His Will no matter what it cost her. Look how it changed her life? She is revered throughout history instead of being a no name in an obscure gene- alogy. One of my favorite Christmas songs is "Mary Did You Know," as it expresses the wonderment of how she must have felt while she was feeding JESUS, WHO IS GOD, Who nursed at her breast, while stroking his baby fine hair back as she held Him and sang to Him. Wow, look at what <u>Obedience</u> brought her, a lot of pain and discomfort, but what tremendous rewards!!!

Let's take a look at Joseph. In that culture, it was extremely important to marry a virgin and now he is looking at his wife like she is a possible adulteress. I can see him pacing his room and thinking through what he just heard from God. "Did I hear that right? God says by a 'Miracle' (not an everyday occurrence then or now) Mary is going to have a baby and I am to live with her and sleep with her and not touch her until the baby is born." Pretty tough for any man, much less one who lived in a culture where marrying a pregnant woman would bring shame to him in front of everyone? People would talk and count the months and come up with "something happened here." The point is that Joseph trusted God and Obeyed Him.

## JOSEPH TRUSTED GOD AND OBEYED

What would have happened if Joseph hadn't obeyed God? God would have chosen another way, but Joseph would have missed the blessing of reaping the rewards of Obedience, and being named for all eternity as the man who OBEYED God and raised "Jesus." Can you imagine raising Jesus who was God and teaching him the ways of life just like any father would, teaching Him his trade and having prayer with Him. Imagine leading GOD in prayer!!!! What a phenomenon! That absolutely blows my mind.

Joseph must have grieved having to transport Mary on a donkey when she was in labor. Ask any mother and you will find out that labor is no fun, much less travelling for hours on the back of a bouncing donkey. As Mary got closer to birthing, Joseph must have gotten more and more desperate as the contractions got closer and closer, and still no place for Mary to lay down to have this child. I wonder if she had second thoughts about what she had agreed to. I bet she didn't bargain on this. We will often find ourselves in a similar mess when we obey God, because the going can get rough and we will be tempted to give up. Once committed to God's plan, Mary didn't have the choice to quit, she was pregnant and abortion was unheard of. I can imagine how desperate they must have been to be willing to lay down in a stable. It wasn't nice and clean as we portray it in our pageants today, but smelled of manure and urine-soaked straw that may not have been cleaned up for awhile. No sterile hospital, no nurses to help clean up, just a bed of hay to birth her child among the animals. (With my love of animals, I couldn't think of a more wonderful place, but I doubt if Mary felt that way.) Birthing is not clean and dry, but is messy no matter how you look at it, so how did they clean it up? How many women today would put up with that even if they knew it was something God wanted? Wow, we would probably say, "What kind of God would do that to someone He loves, especially His own son?"

I wonder what went through their minds when the shepherds came in from the fields. Here Joseph and

Mary were in this stable, probably hadn't had a chance to bathe, or buy baby clothes, and here come the shepherds showing up to worship their baby. (I don't think they took many baths back then, especially when they spent all their time in the fields with their flocks of sheep.) After Joseph and Mary finally procured a house in Nazareth where the three of them moved in, more visitors arrived–the Wise Men, astrologers of that day. I wonder if Mary and Joseph were surprised at these visitors who came to worship Jesus, who was by then at least a toddler, as the Bible says, "the young child."

The whole point I am trying to make is look what happened when two people OBEYED AND TRUSTED GOD. Had they not, look at what they would have missed! Mary would never have had the joy of being so intimate with "God, in human flesh," and Joseph would have missed raising and teaching "God" as his son. I can imagine they were both blown away at how Jesus taught them. I bet they'd tell us that all the hardship was worth it.

I love the way God provided for their needs. Now again, God provides for Joseph even before the need arises and I believe it was because God was preserving

Jesus's life, as well as blessing this couple for their obedience. The Wise Men brought them enough to supply their needs for quite awhile, as frankincense and myrrh were very valuable herbs back then, and of course, gold. God protected the Wise Men (the Bible does not say how many came, but it is nice poetry that we assume three, based on the three kinds of gifts) as they traveled across the orient, especially riding camels. It was a very, very long and dangerous journey in those days. There were an abundance of robbers, and a procession as well-dressed and opulent-looking as this group would have been a target. But God intended those gifts for Mary and Joseph and He didn't allow anything to get in the way of His provision.

Again Joseph heard God in a "dream," and quickly obeyed by taking off for Egypt. How many of you would have responded to a dream telling you to flee the country when there was no obvious reason to go. Only God knew what was coming and even though Joseph didn't, he still obeyed because he trusted the dream sent from God, thus escaping Herod and his soldiers. Would you have faced what Joseph faced based on a dream?

How many times has God provided for us in ways we can't understand, and yet when we hit hard times we fear that He might not be there for us this time? Well, we don't have the Baby Jesus, but we do have Him in our lives and we should be His walking example to the world. That is important to Him. He will provide what we need, when we need it, not necessarily what we want.

I remember one time when visiting in Florida, I met a lady who had a tumor the size of a grapefruit on her shoulder. She, her friends and family, all had been praying that she would be healed, but the tumor remained. When I visited, I offered her a bottle of the Herbal Extract that would have taken it off, but she refused as she only wanted God to miraculously remove it. How many times has God brought you an answer and because it wasn't what you wanted, you refused it? He's already prepared our help, and we just won't see it.

How many times has God put the thought in our minds to do something for someone and we put it off? He will find another way to get His will done, but look at the blessings you will miss in the meantime by not fulfilling His will. God can do anything He wants, but He chooses to do it through us.

## GRAB HIS BLESSINGS WITH OBEDIENCE

The next thing I want to touch on is TIMING. Had Jesus's birth been today what a different outcome! There would be no Wise Men, just an ATM. Mary would have been an unwed mother. No big deal, she would have ridden to the hospital and had Him in a sterile condition, no visitors, just family, the star would have been named by NASA as a new comet or planet and ignored as being from God, and there wouldn't be a Christmas to celebrate. Most important of all, the timing of Jesus's birthday and death had to do with the spread of the Gospel. The apostles were able to cover the "World" with the Gospel of Christ, which was spread as populations grew and moved out over the globe. Look at all the millions of people who would have died without the Knowledge of His saving Grace had He come today. They wouldn't have even covered it as newsworthy on CNN. God has His timing for everything, even the events of our lives. All that is required is OBEDIENCE, SO WE DON'T MISS OUT ON THE BLESSINGS HE INTENDED FOR US. NO TELLING WHAT HE

WILL CALL US TO DO AND WHEN, IF WE JUST
LEARN THAT FACT.

One last thought. Whatever we do, our lives and decisions affect others. The Scriptures are full of examples of the results of obedience and disobedience. Look at Romans 5:19—read how Adam's disobedience affected all of mankind, and Jesus's obedience reversed that for all who accept Him. Abraham disobeyed God and had a child by his wife's handmaiden who bore him Ishmael in direct disobedience to God's command. Later, Isaac was born according to God's Plan and was to be Abraham's only heir, so Abraham sent Ishmael and his mother away. This caused such hatred between their descendents (the Arabs from Ishmael, and the Jews from Isaac) that they have been fighting ever since, resulting in thousands and thousands of horrible deaths and all because of one man's disobedience. The children of Israel have been driven from their land time and time again, because they repeatedly disobeyed God as a nation and they have been slaughtered by the millions as a result of that disobedience. The movie "It's a Wonderful Life," was a great picture of one man's influence. As we look back on our lives and the many crossroads and decisions we've made, I wonder if we will ever know what influence our lives had, or missed, because of obedience or disobedience.

I am so glad Romans 8:28 is as true today as it always has been. "And we know that God causes everything to work together for the good of those who love God and are called according to his purpose for them." Years ago, when I turned my life over to the leading of the Holy Spirit (which is called the Baptism of the Holy Spirit in Charismatic circles), I learned the importance of trusting God no matter what He told me to do. Believe me, some of those things were pretty bazaar; but when I obeyed, I could see the hand of the Lord in it. When I first started out with Animal Communication, it was hard because people made fun of me. But God told me "if you obey me in this and trust me, someday I will justify you," and He did. The rewards have FAR outweighed the criticism and persecution by Christians and non-Christians, because I obeyed Him. The things He called me to do and the things I have accomplished were directly related to obedience to His leading. But my sorrows over the past three years weighed me down, and I lost sight of the Holy Spirit.

I use to approach the Holidays with just the thought of getting them behind me until God opened my eyes to the Obedience and Timing of Christmas. Christmas now takes on a whole new meaning, and I realize He never left me—I took my eyes off of Him and fell into circumstances. I couldn't hear His small voice anymore. I renewed that intimacy this Christmas, and it has been the best Christmas ever. It was filled with going out into the community, listening to Him as He directed me to homes that needed the food I had from the food bank and the bakery, and seeing the rewards of hearts warmed by God's love. I spent the time doing what I could to serve Him and it was exciting, especially now that I understand more of what Christmas is about.

This book has been written to remind me of His perfect Hand in my life, how far I have come and how far I still need to go, just as much as it was written to inspire others to trust Him. I pray that you, too, will step out in obedience to His calling on your life, so that you can enjoy the rewards He will heap on you for so doing. I have lived an incredible life, sometimes exciting and sometimes tough, but obeying Him and His calling on my life has been worth it all. I wouldn't change much even if I could. Look what I would have missed if I hadn't obeyed. I couldn't imagine my life any differently and the rewards have been great. He is so faithful and patient with us. At my age, life is still exciting, has new adventures, and is fulfilling because of what He has led me to understand and experience.

OBEDIENCE is all that is required!

THIS IS THE SECOND MESSAGE OF
CHRISTMAS. ISN'T THAT GREAT?

I Samuel 15:22

OBEDIENCE IS BETTER THAN SACRIFICE.

---

- The experiences that deeply impacted my life while living in town are told in my book, <u>My Journey through the Three Dimensions of Natural Healing.</u>
- This is explained more fully in my book, <u>Seasons, My Journey Through The Three Dimensions Of Natural Healing.</u>

I first began training police dogs when I was with the Yuma, Arizona, Police Department in 1967. I didn't meet Bea Lydecker until several years later, when I was involved in training police dogs in Coos Bay, Oregon. Her insights into animal behavior helped me greatly, and her ability to communicate with the dogs fascinated me. Therefore, I took some classes from her and learned to use her techniques myself. This has been an invaluable help to me in training dogs, and in screening dogs for their suitability for police work. Subsequently, I was able to successfully train many dogs for law enforcement departments in both Oregon and Washington.

My relationship with all animals, as well as with most people, has been enhanced by the skills taught by Bea. She is a generous and kind person who truly loves her fellow beings, regardless of species!

Kimball P. Vickery
Chief of Police, Retired
Mt. Angel, Oregon

In 1969, Bea discovered she had a unique, God-given ability to communicate telepathically with animals and people, Her gift was not well received by fellow Christians until Pastor Jack Hayford brought her into his fold and encouraged her to follow the leading of the Holy Spirit. Today, Bea is endorsed by doctors, veterinarians and educators alike. Her story is told in her book, YOU TOO CAN TALK WITH THE ANIMALS, where she teaches animal language and shows students how to use it to help those who are not able to talk. Bea is a renowned Animal Communicator, as well as a lecturer on holistic animal and human nutrition. She has appeared on Oprah Winfrey, David Letterman, Johnny Carson, and Joan Rivers. Articles have been written about her work in publications such as The Wall Street Journal, L.A. Times, Dog World, Cat Fancy, and People Magazine.

www.BeaLydecker.com

CPSIA information can be obtained at www.ICGtesting.com
Printed in the USA
BVOW04s1706240914

368095BV00005B/17/P